JAMES BARBER
THE URBAN PEASANT

COOKING
for TWO

HARBOUR PUBLISHING

to Christina

Harbour Publishing
PO Box 219
Madeira Park, BC
Canada V0N 2H0
www.harbourpublishing.com

Text design: Counterpunch/Linda Gustafson
Interior photographs: John Sherlock
Cover photograph: Vici Johnstone
Cover design & styling: Anna Comfort
Printed in Canada

Harbour Publishing acknowledges financial support from the Government of Canada through the Book Publishing Industry Development Program and from the Province of British Columbia through the BC Arts Council and the Book Publishing Tax Credit.

BRITISH
COLUMBIA
ARTS COUNCIL
Supported by the Province of British Columbia

Enormous thanks to Anik See

Library and Archives Canada Cataloguing in Publication

Barber, James, 1923–
    Cooking for two / James Barber. — 1st Harbour Pub. ed.

Includes index.
ISBN 978-1-55017-416-8

    1. Cookery for two. 2. Quick and easy cookery. I. Title.

TX714.B3647 2007   641.5'612   C2007-900185-8

CONTENTS

INTRODUCTION

Cooking, like sex and dancing, is a pleasure best shared. This is a book about what two people can do with their own four hands, and not a lot of time. It's also a book about pleasure. Two people in the kitchen can have as much fun as two people in the bath.

The gourmet cookbooks and the glossy magazines with their beautiful pictures always assume that cooking is a solitary and precise occupation for celibate interior decorators, with recipes as rigid as drugstore prescriptions, and their cooking becomes a joyless duty, when it ought to be a shared courtship, a foreplay to the intimacy of a shared dinner. "Let's cook supper" will do a lot more for your relationship than "I'm cooking. Leave me alone." And if you're making this supper for just the two of you, there's no reason why the bath, or a rug by the fire, shouldn't become an occasional part of the recipe. One of the most important ingredients of most good cooking is time – a little while for everything in the pot to settle down and adjust, to balance and smooth out. You don't have to stand there and worry about it, or keep dabbing with a spoon – it just happens.

And you don't have to worry about what it will taste like: when two people are involved, it always tastes good. They don't have to be lovers – there's nothing more rewarding than cooking with a three-year-old, unless it's skating around the back end of an eighty-year-old gran, watching how she makes the recipe she somehow can't write down for you.

Cooking for two is very intimate and very immediate. I very seldom start to cook for a guest until the doorbell rings, and then we do it together. Of course you can't both hold the knife to chop parsley, nor can you both stir a sauce with the same spoon. But what you can do and will find yourselves doing, if you cook together, is *dancing*. That's exactly what it is: learning to move and accommodate one another, learning to enjoy one another's peculiarities and discovering the pleasures of unspoken communication. I can remember a bottle of very expensive balsamic vinegar (small, like a perfume bottle, and $375 — it was a birthday gift) that I kept unopened just because it was such a treasure, such an exotic. She'd come to supper — she said she couldn't cook — and she was fascinated with the little bottle, that anything so small could cost so much. She didn't say, but she obviously wanted to open it, so I sliced her some white peaches and right there and then watched her turn into a cook. Carefully as a newly ordained priest, she anointed those peaches, drop by drop, and when we ate them she looked as pleased as a preschooler with a valentine card for mum (or a chicken that's just laid its first egg?), and that's really what cooking together is all about. Everything tastes so much better if you've both had your fingers in the pot.

The recipes in this book are basically simple. Very few of them take more than half an hour to get on the table. They're meant for two people with good appetites, but if you both feel dainty one evening, there may be leftovers for the office lunch. Half a dozen of them are recipes from earlier books, old favourites that I consider essential to anybody beginning to cook. I try to minimize the number of pots and pans, and I try to use ingredients that are readily available in most corner stores. Flowers are nice on the table, and music helps, but the best beginning of any dinner is the symphony of smells and anticipation that builds itself around the two of you.

APPETIZERS

*S*mell is the real appetizer.

We like to think we fall in love with brains, or beauty, or a voice. We want love to be something more than the animal, something more socially acceptable than animal passion. And so we are pushovers for the *saniteers*, those one-dimensional perfectionists who live in an emotional carwash, thinking that a shining, undented life is a perfect life, and basing the value of everything they see or touch on how *clean* it is.

They show us pictures in glossy magazines, with centrefolds of airbrushed beauties and plates of impossible food, one as intimidating as the other. We watch television — all those people with perfect teeth, zitless complexions and ever-smiling happiness, all driving (in sunshine) the latest, gleamingest cars. And these become our icons, our ambitions, just because it's very hard to resist all those commercials that cost millions of dollars to make. Say something loud enough and long enough, and at least half the world will believe it's true. Suddenly we start to believe that neat and clean and tidy are not only desirable, but essential. Life and love are painted by numbers. Everything that isn't perfect ought to be, and far too many things (and people) are rejected because they don't fit into the scrubbed and scoured perfection of the marketing managers.

But real life is a messy business, and it smells. Smell is really what we fall in love with. We may not realize it, and most of us don't want to accept it, but smell is what drags us across the room at a party to make our pass. Smell is the first sense we're born with, the sense that automatically turns a baby's head to its mother for the first feed of its life. Smell is what warns us of fires in hotels. All good kitchens smell. Real estate agents know that houses with cookies baking in the oven sell quicker than those that are scrubbed, aired out and sanitized until they look like operating theatres. Smell is comfort and familiarity, but at the same time it's the first of the warning signs. It's basic and primitive: the ancients knew that a bad smell usually meant danger and signalled a need for caution.

Smell is what appreciating wine is all about, and the same sense of smell (even if you do get all scientific and call it pheromones) is what leads you to your own true love.

But we've learned to spray ourselves, turn on the fan, open the windows and refuse to eat garlic at lunch-time. Old people live in retirement homes designed by architects who think that residents need (and want) to be alone. Most of them are not just alone — they're lonely. I teach them to fry onions on the stove, and open the door to the hallway. They're nearly always surprised at how quickly their neighbours drop by to introduce themselves and then stay to make friends, and a lot of them decide that cooking for two is a lot more fun than living in smell-less solitude.

Smell is the best appetizer.

Baked Olives

Dead easy.

1	clove garlic	1
1 cup	large black or green pitted olives	250 mL
¼ cup	white wine	50 mL

*W*hile your oven preheats to 350°F (180°C), chop the garlic. Place the olives, wine and chopped garlic in greased baking dish, and bake, uncovered, for 15–20 minutes. Remove them from the oven, let them sit for 5 minutes and serve.

Russian Egg Salad

Party food – you can boil the eggs the night before.

2	eggs	2
	A handful of walnuts	
	A sprig of dill	
	A pinch of salt	
2 tbsp	hot pepper relish or salsa	25 mL

*W*hile you hard-boil the eggs, have someone finely chop the walnuts and dill. When the eggs are done, let them sit under cold running water until cool. Peel the eggs, and chop them. Add the remaining ingredients and serve. In winter you'll have to use dried dill.

Potatoes with Walnuts and Yogurt

2	large potatoes	2
	A handful of walnuts	
½ cup	yogurt	125 mL
	A few sprigs of cilantro	
	Salt	
	Pepper	

While you chop the potatoes into bite-sized pieces and put them on to boil, have someone else toast the walnuts in a dry frypan over high heat. When they are done, let them cool, and then chop them. When the potatoes are done, drain them and toss them immediately with the walnuts and yogurt. Tear the cilantro leaves into coarse pieces, and sprinkle them over the potatoes. Season with salt and pepper, and serve.

Garlic Mushrooms

Don't forget the salt.	2 tbsp	butter	25 mL
	⅔ lb	mushrooms	350 g
	1	clove garlic	1
		A sprig of parsley	
		A squeeze of lemon juice	
		Salt	
		Pepper	

*W*hile you melt the butter in a frypan over medium heat, have some-one wash the mushrooms and chop the garlic and parsley. Add the mushrooms and garlic to the pan, and cook for 5–6 minutes, stirring. Add the lemon juice, and cook for a further 2 minutes, lid on. Sprinkle with parsley, season with salt and pepper, and serve.

Stuffed Tomatoes

2	eggs	2
1	tin (4 oz/113 g) baby shrimp	1
	2 tomatoes	2
2 tbsp	mayonnaise	25 mL
	Zest of ½ lemon	
	Salt	
	Pepper	

While you hard-boil the eggs, have someone drain and rinse the shrimp. Cut the tops of the tomatoes off, and scoop out the insides. Place the tomato flesh in a bowl, and mix it with the mayonnaise, shrimp and lemon zest. When the eggs are cooked, drain them and let them sit under cold running water until cool. Peel, chop and add them to the shrimp mixture. Season the shrimp mixture with salt and pepper, and stuff it into the tomato shells. Serve.

Sicilian Pumpkin with Mint

Perfect for a fall party.

2 tbsp	vegetable oil	25 mL
½ lb	pumpkin or squash	250 g
1	clove garlic	1
	A sprig of mint	
	A pinch of white sugar	
	Salt	
	Pepper	

hile you heat the oil in a frypan over medium-high heat, have someone slice the pumpkin into ½-inch (1 cm) thick pieces. Add the pumpkin to the frypan, and cook for 6 minutes. In the meantime, chop the garlic and mint. Turn the slices of pumpkin over, and add the garlic and sugar. Cook for 6 more minutes, until the pumpkin is tender and cooked through. Serve sprinkled with the chopped mint, and salt and pepper to taste.

Catalan-Style Bruschetta

½	crusty French baguette	½	Works fine in a
1	tomato	1	toaster oven.
2 tbsp	Parmesan cheese	25 mL	
	A sprig of basil or tarragon, chopped		

While your broiler preheats, cut the bread into thin slices, and have someone cut the tomato in half. Rub each slice of bread with the cut tomato and sprinkle the bread with some cheese. Broil for 2–3 minutes, until the cheese has melted, and serve topped with chopped basil.

Turkish Eggplant Sandwiches

Supper turns into
a party for two.

¼ cup	vegetable oil	50 mL
2 oz	feta cheese	50 g
4	slices eggplant, each ½ inch (1 cm) thick	4
¼ cup	bread crumbs	50 mL
1	egg	1

Heat the oil in a frypan over medium-high heat. While you assemble one sandwich, have someone assemble the other. Crumble half of the cheese over one slice of the eggplant. Place another slice of eggplant on top, to make a sandwich. Place the bread crumbs in a shallow dish, and beat the egg in another shallow dish until it has a uniform colour. Dip the sandwich in the egg, and then in the bread crumbs, coating both sides. Place the sandwich in the frypan. Make another sandwich with the remaining ingredients, and place it in the frypan too. Cook the sandwiches for 4–5 minutes on each side, until the cheese has melted and the eggplant is cooked. Serve immediately.

Salmon-Stuffed olives

1	tin (6 ½ oz/184 g) salmon	1		Slightly messy but worth it.
3 tbsp	mayonnaise	45 mL		
	A squeeze of lemon juice			
	Pepper			
24	large green pitted olives	24		

*D*rain the salmon, and place it in a small bowl. Mix it together with the mayonnaise, lemon juice, and pepper to taste. Stuff the holes in the olives with the salmon mixture, and serve. Also works well with tuna or smoked-salmon flavoured cream cheese.

Scallop and Potato Flan

Someone always gives ramekins at weddings.

4	new potatoes, boiled	4	
4 oz	scallops	100 g	
	Salt		
	Pepper		
	A dollop of butter		
1	lemon	1	
	A sprig of parsley		
¼	tomato	¼	

*P*reheat your oven to 375°F (190°C). Peel the potatoes, and slice thinly. While you butter two 1-cup (250 mL) ramekins, have someone slice the scallops into thin rounds. Arrange a layer of potatoes on the bottom of each ramekin, and season lightly with salt and pepper. Arrange a layer of scallops over the potatoes, and finish with a second layer of potatoes. Season lightly with salt and pepper, and drop a dollop of butter on top. Cut the lemon into six slices, and arrange them in a layer on top of the butter. Bake, uncovered, for 15 minutes or until bubbling. Have someone chop the parsley and cut the tomato into small cubes. When the flans have finished baking, flip them upside down on a plate, and garnish with parsley and tomato.

Roasted Garlic

2	medium heads garlic	2
1 tbsp	olive oil	15 mL
1 tsp	white wine	5 mL
½ tsp	white sugar	2 mL
	Salt	
	Pepper	
4 oz	goat's cheese	100 g
	Some very good bread	

Preheat your oven to 400°F (200°C). While you are preparing the garlic, have someone set up the plates. Chop the tops off the garlic, exposing the tops of the cloves. Drizzle 1 tsp (5 mL) of the olive oil and wine over the top, and then sprinkle with the sugar and season lightly with salt and pepper. Bake the garlic in an ungreased baking pan for 25 minutes or until the heads are nicely browned and the cloves look ready to pop. To set up the plates, portion the cheese onto two plates, drizzle with the remaining olive oil and sprinkle with pepper. Serve the garlic hot from the oven with the cheese, smearing both onto thick pieces of very good bread.

SOUPS

*E*ating wasn't much fun in the early days. Roots in the ground, berries on the trees or clams on the beach. If you were lucky, a slab off a sabre-toothed tiger — you found it, chewed it and swallowed it. Raw. When fire was discovered, things changed a bit. You found it, burned it and then chewed it and swallowed it. If you ran out of teeth (a fairly common thing to run out of, according to the archaeologists), you learned to go hungry, until somebody (a woman with a toothless husband?) discovered that heating in water tenderized food more than burning, and with less effort. At first they dumped hot rocks in animal hides and wooden boxes and anything else that would hold water. Then somebody found that it was easier to heat the water in a clay pot, right on the fire, and so it went, all the way to copper pots, nonstick frypans, Martha Stewart and orthodontics.

But the really important thing that came from all this culinary evolution wasn't cookware. One horribly cold night somebody needing a drink didn't want to go out of the cave to the stream, dipped a cup of the water out of the cooking pot (the water with the meat and vegetables cooking in it) and liked it. Nice. It made her feel good. Next day she gave some to the kids, along with the meat and veg, and they liked it. So did the toothless husband. And soup was invented. But even more important, so was stock, which, despite all the wonderfully complicated recipes in the fancy cookbooks, is no more than water enriched by simmering things in it — the easiest of all kitchen tricks and the most rewarding.

There are very few things that stock won't improve. Vegetables, stews, beans, lentils, rice — they all benefit from the extra flavour and extra richness that comes from this enriched liquid. And the making of stock is ridiculously easy because it makes itself while you do something else. Stock cubes are a last resort. A lot of restaurants have a stockpot on a low flame all night — nobody watches it, nobody worries.

You can do exactly the same, or you can let it simmer while you go to a movie, watch the box, make love or sweep the dustballs from under the bed. Saturday afternoons in winter are my favourite times for making stock — everybody else is skiing or getting cold standing around garage sales, but we've got feet up, books to read, tea and chocolate biscuits while the stockpot quietly bubbles.

Water, bones, onions and carrots are the basics for stock. There is no single recipe, although you'll find all kinds of cookbooks insisting not only that you roast the bones but that you only use bones from pedigreed animals of superior intelligence. Ignore them. Restaurants make stock that way, but restaurants have people to clean their ovens and scrub their pans. All you need is a large pot, with three or four tablespoons of oil in it. Heat the pot over high heat, and add three chopped onions. Stir them occasionally while you slice or dice a bunch of carrots, and add the carrots to the pot when the onions smell sweet and sugary.

Now add three or four pounds of bones (chicken backs, necks and feet usually have meat on them, and they're inexpensive). Add water to within an inch of the top, bring it to the boil and immediately turn down the heat to simmer. Skim the sludge off the top once or twice, partially cover with the lid and let it simmer for three, four or five hours, adding half a cup of water occasionally. Turn off the heat, and let it cool overnight on the balcony or outside the back door (but put the lid on – mice and birds like stock). Lift the fat off, pour the stock into small plastic containers, label it and freeze. Or pour it into ice-cube trays, freeze and then dump the cubes into resealable freezer bags.

You will now have stock for a couple of months, which means soup in 10 minutes, wonderful risotto, great beans (cooked in half stock, half water), and whenever you want to be particularly and immediately nice to your significant other. . .

Basic Stock

1	chicken carcass	1	
	(or 1 lb/450 g of leftover chicken bones)		
1	leek	1	
1	large carrot	1	
	Skin of 2 onions, if you have them		
	(if not, the leek will do just fine)		
1	bay leaf	1	
1 tbsp	peppercorns	15 mL	
	A handful of parsley		
1	stalk celery	1	
	(or 1 tbsp/15 mL celery salt)		
	Water		

Every time I make chicken, I freeze the leftover bones, skin and carcass until I need to make stock. I do that with onion skins too, and the butt ends of carrots and leeks.

*P*lace all of the ingredients in a large pot (the bigger the better), and fill the pot with enough water to reach a couple of inches over the chicken carcass. Bring to a rolling boil over medium heat, and use a spoon to remove any scum that may have collected. Reduce the heat to as low as possible and let the stock simmer overnight, or keep the heat at medium and allow the stock to cook for 3 hours or so, until it has a nice yellow colour. Pour the stock through a fine strainer and into small containers for freezing. If you like your stock strong, cook the reduced stock over medium heat for another 40 minutes or so. A great thing to do while watching football on a Sunday afternoon.

Squash Soup

1 tbsp	cumin seeds or ground cumin	15 mL
1	small onion	1
2	cloves garlic	2
1 ⅓ lb	squash	675 g
	(about 2 cups/500 mL chopped)	
2 tbsp	vegetable oil	25 mL
3 cups	chicken stock	750 mL
2 tbsp	butter	25 mL
½ cup	light cream	125 mL
	Salt	
	Pepper	

Toast the cumin seeds in a dry pot over medium heat until you can smell their spiciness. In the meantime, have someone chop the onion and garlic, and peel and chop the squash into bite-sized pieces. Add the oil to the pot, and wait a minute for it to heat up. Add the onion and garlic, and cook for 3–4 minutes, until the onion starts to turn clear. Increase the heat to high, and add the cumin, stock and squash. Bring to a boil, and let it all cook for 15–20 minutes, until the squash is tender. Purée the soup in a food processor or with a hand blender (if the soup is too thick, add water or more stock). When the soup is smooth, return it to the pot, and stir in the butter. Gradually add the cream, season with salt and pepper, and serve.

Cold Tomato, Lemon and Couscous Soup

2 tbsp	vegetable oil	25 mL
1	small onion	1
1	clove garlic	1
3	tomatoes	3
1	sweet red pepper	1
1 ½ cups	water	375 mL
½ cup	couscous	125 mL
	A sprig of fresh mint	
	Zest of ½ lemon	
½ cup	yogurt	125 mL
	Salt	
	Pepper	

Heat the oil in a saucepan over medium-high heat while someone chops the onion, garlic, tomatoes and red pepper. Add the chopped vegetables to the saucepan, and cook for 3 minutes. Add the water, and bring it to a boil. Stir in the couscous, turn the heat off, cover the saucepan and let the couscous sit for 5–10 minutes, until it absorbs most of the moisture. Chop the mint, stir it into the couscous with the lemon zest and yogurt, and put the whole thing in the fridge for half an hour or so while you cut the lawn or do your nails or call your mum. Season with salt and pepper and serve. Lovely in the heat of summer. . .

Canned Clam Chowder for Two

4	slices bacon	4
1	small onion	1
2	cloves garlic	2
2	small potatoes	2
	A few sprigs of parsley	
1 tbsp	flour	15 mL
1 cup	water	250 mL
1	bay leaf	1
2 cups	clam nectar or juice	500 mL
1	tin (5 oz/142 g) small clams	1
½ cup	whipping cream	250 mL
	Salt	
	Pepper	

Slice the bacon into small pieces while you heat a large saucepan over medium-high heat. Add the bacon to the saucepan, and have some-one look after it (stirring it once in awhile so it doesn't burn) while you chop the onion, garlic, potato (skin on, into bite-sized pieces) and parsley. When the bacon is crisp, add the onion and garlic, cook-ing for 2 minutes or until the onion has turned clear. In the mean-time, place the flour in a cup, and stir some of the water into it until it is smooth (no lumps!). Add the potatoes, bay leaf, water and flour, and clam nectar to the pot, and bring it all to a boil while someone rinses and drains the clams. Let the soup cook for 10 minutes or so, and then stir in the clams, parsley and cream. Discard the bay leaf, season with salt and pepper, and serve.

Green Bean, Mint and Rice Soup

2 tbsp	vegetable oil	25 mL
1	small onion	1
1	clove garlic	1
	A handful of green beans	
3 cups	chicken stock	750 mL
⅓ cup	uncooked long-grain rice	75 mL
	A sprig of mint	
	Salt	
	Pepper	

Heat the oil in a saucepan over medium-high heat while someone chops the onion and garlic, and cuts the ends off the beans. Add the onion to the saucepan, and cook for 3 minutes. Add the garlic, and cook for 2 minutes while someone cuts the green beans into bite-sized pieces. Stir the stock into the saucepan, and bring to a boil. Reduce the heat to low, add the rice and allow the mixture to simmer for 15 minutes or so, or until the rice is almost done and the soup has turned a little thick. Add the beans, and cook for 5 more minutes. Just before serving, chop the mint, and season the soup with salt and pepper. Serve the soup with the chopped mint sprinkled over top.

Quick Potato and Pasta Soup

Neapolitan soul
food.

1	small onion	1
1	tomato	1
1	small potato	1
2 tbsp	vegetable oil	25 mL
4 cups	chicken stock	1 L
	A pinch of red pepper flakes	
	A handful of uncooked macaroni	
	or other smallish pasta	
	A handful of parsley	
	Salt	
	Pepper	
	Sour cream	

While you chop the onion, tomato and potato into small pieces, have someone heat the oil in a saucepan over medium-high heat. Add the onion to the saucepan, and cook for 5 minutes. Add the tomato and potato to the saucepan, stir it all about and then pour in the stock. Bring the mixture to a boil, and then add the red pepper flakes and pasta. Cook the soup until the potato is tender, about 15 minutes. In the meantime, chop the parsley, and set the table. Season the soup with salt and pepper, and serve it with a sprinkling of the chopped parsley and a dollop of sour cream.

Cold Carrot, Ginger and Lime Soup

2 tbsp	vegetable oil	25 mL	Summer,
4	large carrots	4	Summer,
½ inch	fresh ginger	1 cm	Summer.
1	small green chili pepper	1	
1 cup	chicken stock	250 mL	
	Juice of 2 limes		
1 cup	buttermilk	250 mL	
	(or 1 cup/250 mL milk		
	mixed with the juice of 1 lime)		
	Salt		
	Pepper		

Heat the oil in a saucepan over medium-high heat. In the meantime, have someone grate the carrots and ginger, and chop the chili pepper. Add the carrots and ginger to the saucepan, and cook for 2 minutes or until the carrots start to caramelize. Stir in the stock, and bring the mixture to a boil. Reduce the heat to low, and cook for 7–8 minutes, until the carrots are tender. Add the chopped chili pepper, lime juice and buttermilk, and purée the mixture in a food processor or with a hand blender until smooth. Season with salt and pepper, let it cool and serve (it's also delicious hot).

AVGOLEMONO

A Greek soup that's pure ecstasy.	3	eggs	3
	¼ cup	fresh lemon juice	50 mL
	1 ½ cups	chicken stock	375 mL
		Salt	

*W*hile you beat the eggs and lemon juice together until frothy, have someone warm the stock up, without letting it boil. Pour the egg mixture into the stock while whisking constantly (so that the eggs don't curdle). Season with salt, and serve immediately.

STRACCIATELLA

Italian eggdrop soup.	1	egg	1
	2 tbsp	grated Parmesan cheese	25 mL
		A couple of sprigs of parsley	
	3 cups	chicken stock	750 mL
		A pinch of nutmeg	

*W*hile you beat the egg and cheese together, have someone chop the parsley and warm up the stock. When the stock is steaming (but not boiling), remove it from the heat, and stir the egg mixture into it. Serve immediately, sprinkling each bowl with chopped parsley and a pinch of nutmeg.

Turkish Cold Yogurt Soup

2 tbsp	walnuts	25 mL
1	clove garlic	1
½	long English cucumber	½
	A couple of sprigs of mint	
1 cup	yogurt	250 mL
	Ice water	
	Salt	
	Pepper	

*W*hile you toast the walnuts in a dry frypan, have someone mince the garlic, cucumber and mint. Allow the walnuts to cool, and then chop them. Combine the walnuts, garlic, cucumber, mint and yogurt in a bowl, and refrigerate for 3 hours. Just before serving, add enough ice water to thin the soup to the consistency of a thin pancake batter. Season with salt and pepper, and serve. Terrific on hot summer days when even the cicadas are sweating.

Tomato and Bread Soup

¼ cup	good olive oil	50 mL
1	small onion	1
2	cloves garlic	2
1 lb	very ripe tomatoes (about 3 medium)	450 g
	A couple of sprigs of basil	
1 tsp	salt	5 mL
¾ cup	bread crumbs	175 mL
	Grated Parmesan cheese	

*W*hile you heat the oil in a saucepan over medium heat, have someone chop the onion, garlic, tomatoes and basil. Add the onions and garlic to the pan, and cook, stirring, until softened and clear, about 10 minutes. Add the tomatoes and salt, and cook for 20 minutes, until the tomatoes have collapsed. For a smooth soup, purée the mixture in a food processor and return it to the saucepan. For a chunkier soup, leave it as it is. Turn off the heat, and stir the bread crumbs in. Let the soup sit for 10 minutes, and then serve with chopped basil and Parmesan cheese sprinkled over top. Good hot or cold.

WATERCRESS SOUP

½	leek, white part only	½
1	head watercress	1
2 tbsp	butter	25 g
2 cups	chicken stock	500 mL
1 tbsp	fresh lemon juice	15 mL
¼ cup	whipping cream	50 mL
	Salt	
	Pepper	

CROUTONS

1	crusty bun	1
1	clove garlic	1
1 tsp	olive oil	5 mL

*P*reheat your oven to 350°F (180°C). While you are making the soup, have someone prepare the croutons. Carefully wash the leek, and then roughly chop the leek and watercress. Sauté them in butter over medium heat, and then cover with the chicken stock and lemon juice. Bring to a boil, and then reduce to simmer for 5 minutes. Purée the soup in a food processor or blender until smooth, and then return it to the pot and add the cream. Gently heat, and season with salt and pepper. To make the croutons, cut the bun into rounds, and then peel and crush the garlic clove with the broad side of your knife. Rub the clove into the bread, brush the bread with olive oil and season lightly with salt and pepper. Toast on the middle rack of your oven until golden on all sides, about 8 minutes.

EGGS AND CHEESE

*E*ggs are the most versatile of all things in the kitchen. They make cooking a pleasure rather than an obligation, and may be one of the first reasons to consider staying put, in the same place with the same person. I like to think of the first settlers (it doesn't matter where they settled): they all made a simple bread, a sort of bannock, out of flour and water. One day an egg fell in the dough, and it tasted so much better that they did it again and decided to settle down and raise chickens so they could always have an egg in the bread. Two eggs were even better, and three made it a cake. Next thing you know, they were getting married, having brunches, putting in hot tubs, designing gourmet kitchens and buying omelette pans.

Eggs are the first thing to learn to cook in the kitchen, and the first thing to learn about eggs is how to make an omelette. Even more important is how to make your omelette light and fluffy. The trick is to add half an eggshell of cold water to three eggs, with half a teaspoon each of salt and pepper, and a good pinch of cayenne. Nothing else. Beat them lightly (they should still look a little stringy) while you heat a nonstick pan over high heat.

When the pan is hot (flick water on it and if the drops bounce in little balls then it's hot enough), add a good tablespoon of butter, swirl it around to coat the pan and immediately add the eggs. Stir the eggs vigorously with a fork held flat in the pan until the bottom sets, and then cook for a minute more. Tip the pan towards a plate, lift the back third of the omelette and fold it over the middle third. Then roll the whole thing out onto the plate, the bottom lightly browned and the middle soft and sensuous (it continues to cook while you bring it to the table, so don't let it get hard in the pan). Water and high heat are the secrets, and once you get used to it you can make a great omelette in less than 2 minutes. This also means dinner in 2 minutes — just enough time for the significant other to light the candles.

Always have a few eggs in the fridge — hard-boiled or raw. They are not only the quickest meal you can make, but the most comforting and the most comfortable. They're easy and forgiving, and they'll settle down with almost anything. Suddenly you find that a frittata is easy, and so is a Tortilla Español. Scrambled eggs are fine with asparagus, but if you can't  find asparagus, they're almost as good with green beans, cooked just as you would the asparagus. Cook them simply, cook them quickly and don't let things get too complicated. Eggs Benedict is for the professionals. Romance, by definition, is for amateurs.

Basic Omelette

2 tbsp	butter	25 mL
3	eggs	3
1 tbsp	water	15 mL
	A pinch of salt	
	A pinch of pepper	

*W*hile you melt the butter in a frypan over medium heat, have someone crack the eggs into a large bowl with the water, salt and pepper
and beat them until they are a uniform colour. Pour the eggs into
the pan, and with a fork, stir the eggs in a circular motion for a
minute or so. Then let the eggs cook without stirring until they look
almost done. Loosen the edge of one side of the omelette, and fold it
in half. Slide the omelette onto a plate, and eat immediately.

Baked Cheese

A great appetizer!

4 oz	feta or goat's cheese	100 g
1 tbsp	good olive oil	15 mL
½ tsp	red pepper flakes	2 mL
	Pepper	

*P*reheat your oven to 400°F (200°C). Cut the cheese into ½-inch
(1 cm) thick slices and place them in an ungreased baking dish. Drizzle with half of the olive oil, and sprinkle with the red pepper flakes
and pepper. Bake, uncovered until just melted, about 8–10 minutes.
Serve with the remaining olive oil drizzled over top.

Tortilla Español

2 tbsp	olive oil	25 mL
1	small potato	1
1	small onion	1
4	eggs	4
1 tsp	salt	5 mL
½ tsp	pepper	2 mL

Heat the oil in a frypan over medium heat. While you dice the potato and onion into small pieces, have someone beat the eggs, salt and pepper together in a large bowl until smooth. Add the chopped onion and potato to the pan, and cook, stirring occasionally, until the potatoes are tender, about 10 minutes or so. Reduce the heat to low, and pour the beaten eggs over the cooked potato mixture. Cover the frypan. Pour yourselves a glass of wine, and let the "tortilla" cook for 10 minutes or until the top is firm. Remove the lid, and invert a plate over the frypan. Flip the frypan over so the tortilla drops onto the plate, and slide the tortilla back into the frypan. Cook for 2 more minutes, uncovered. Serve wedges of the tortilla hot, cold or lukewarm.

Eggs Piperade

This is called "Chakchouka" in Algeria.	2 tbsp	olive oil	25 mL
	1	clove garlic	1
	1	sweet red pepper	1
	1	sweet green pepper	1
	1	tomato	1
		A couple of sprigs of parsley	
	2	eggs	2
		Salt	
		Pepper	

While you heat the oil in a frypan over medium-high heat, have some-one chop the garlic, peppers, tomato and parsley. Add the chopped vegetables and parsley to the frypan and cook, stirring, for 8 minutes, until the peppers have lost their firmness. With your stirring spoon, make two holes in the vegetable mixture, and crack an egg into each hole. Reduce the heat to medium, cover the pan and let the eggs cook until set, about 4 minutes. Season with salt and pepper, and serve.

Baked Eggs, Bulgarian Style

1 tbsp	olive oil	15 mL
1	tomato	1
4 oz	feta cheese	100 g
2	eggs	2
	A pinch of paprika	
	A pinch of salt	
	A pinch of pepper	
	A sprig of oregano	

Preheat your oven to 350°F (180°C). Pour the olive oil into a cold ovenproof frypan or baking dish while someone else slices the tomato. Place the slices of tomato into the frypan, and crumble half of the feta cheese over top. Break the two eggs over the tomato and feta, and sprinkle with the remaining feta, paprika, salt and pepper. Bake, uncovered, until the eggs are set and the feta has melted, about 10 minutes. In the meantime, chop the fresh oregano. Just before serving, sprinkle the oregano over top.

THE ULTIMATE CHIPS AND DIP

8 oz	*feta or goat's cheese*	*250 g*
¼ cup	*olive oil*	*50 mL*
½	*lemon*	*½*
½ tsp	*red pepper flakes*	*2 mL*
	Pepper	
	Black olives	
	Pita bread	

While you place the cheese and 3 tbsp (45 mL) of the olive oil in a food processor, have someone grate the zest of the half of the lemon. Add the lemon zest to the food processor, and squeeze the juice of the lemon into it as well. Purée until smooth. Transfer the mixture to a serving bowl, and stir in the red pepper flakes and pepper to taste. Drizzle the remaining olive oil over top just before serving. Serve with the olives and wedges of pita bread. For a thicker "dip," refrigerate the cheese mixture for several hours or overnight. Keeps in the fridge for about a week.

Cheese Soufflé

3 tbsp	grated Parmesan cheese	45 mL
1 tsp	butter	5 mL
1 tsp	flour	5 mL
¼ cup	milk	50 mL
2	egg yolks	2
3	egg whites	3
	A pinch of salt	
	A pinch of cream of tartar	
	A pinch of nutmeg	
2 oz	old cheddar cheese	50 g

Preheat your oven to 400°F (200°C). While one of you butters two
1½ cup (375 mL) soufflé dishes and coats the inside of each with 1 tsp
(5 mL) of the Parmesan cheese, the other can cook the butter with the
flour over medium heat until it turns pale blond. Stir in the milk a
little at a time, and continue stirring until the sauce has a smooth,
thick consistency. While you remove the thickened sauce from the
heat and blend in the egg yolks, one at a time, have someone whip the
egg whites with the salt and cream of tartar until stiff peaks form. Stir
the nutmeg, remaining Parmesan cheese and cheddar cheese into the
egg mixture. Fold in one-third of the egg whites, and then fold in the
rest. Spoon the mixture into the two soufflé dishes, and bake, uncovered, on the bottom rack of the oven for 10–12 minutes or until the
soufflés are golden on top and have risen. Serve immediately. Fresh
out of the oven, they are as light as air but they collapse in a breath.

PASTA

"Needs more salt?"

"Think so?"

"Yup."

"Okay."

You don't have to hold hands all the time you're cooking together. But you do have to talk, or grunt, or even practice the Italian you're learning for next year's vacation. Somehow you have to communicate, to decide, to agree — it's what the church calls communion, as an idea translates itself into a special magic. Cooking is an easy magic, an everyday magic that transforms the ordinary, simple stuff of life into a special and joyous shared experience.

Most of this magic has to do with flavours. Pepper and salt are the basics, onions are essential and garlic becomes a habit. A little wine, in a glass or in the cooking pot, improves most dishes. Plain old vanilla ice cream zipped up with a tablespoon of booze (whisky, rum, fancy cognac or vintage port, whatever you've got), suddenly becomes a favourite dessert. Grating a little chocolate (I've used a frozen Mars bar with considerable success) over a sliced orange is a ridiculously simple one-minute trick to end a dinner, and equally simple is learning that most fried things (chicken, fish, even tofu) are dramatically improved by a sprinkle of lemon juice just before they come out of the pan.

The best way to learn flavours is to concentrate on one at a time. The worst thing you can do is buy a spice rack, fully stocked with little jars of spices, most of which will lose all their taste before you get around to using them. Much better to look for one herb, fresh or dried, take it home and use it for a week until you come to understand its essence — how it tastes with the things you regularly cook. You'll make the odd mistake ("Let's not do that again"), but you'll learn to cook in the process and — most important — learn not to be totally dependent on recipes.

Artists learn new colours this way (Picasso had his blue period) and musicians learn new riffs (Louis Armstrong's childhood breakthrough was discovering — and for a long time using only — the black keys). Very simple.

Herbs are just as simple. They separate into two categories: hot and sweet. Thyme, marjoram, rosemary and oregano are the best known of the hot ones. If you don't have thyme, use one of the other hot ones. The French use thyme because it grows wild on sunny banks, the Italians use oregano for the same reason and the Spanish use rosemary with orange zest. Marjoram is really a milder form of oregano, a hot one without the intensity. Whichever you choose, your pasta sauce won't know the difference.

Tarragon, basil and mint are sweet herbs, and nine times out of ten they're also interchangeable. Basil has a smoothness that makes good pesto sauce, but any one of them goes very well with fish or chicken or tofu, especially if you add a splash of white wine in the last couple of minutes of your cooking. They all make a nice herbal tea (add honey to sweeten it while it's still hot, and keep it in the fridge for the next sunny afternoon). Basil goes well with chicken or fish. So does mint and so does tarragon. Each time you get something different. Nine times out of ten you'll like it, possibly even prefer it, but most of all you'll enjoy discovering something new. Slavishly following recipes is like painting by numbers: it can get very dull.

My favourite all-purpose spice is ginger. I use it with chicken, fish and stir-fried vegetables (asparagus, eggplant, cabbage and almost any Chinese vegetable). Poached pears, rhubarb and cooked apples go very well with grated ginger, as do pork chops and tofu and thinly sliced beef. I called my first cookbook *Ginger Tea Makes Friends,* after an Indonesian friend showed me how to make a lovely, comforting tea from fresh ginger and honey. Ever since, I've found ginger as necessary to my cooking as garlic. Even the smallest corner store seems to sell it these days. The trick is to buy it fresh and plump, with the skin all shiny, and use it before it dries out. If you have a great big lump, cut it into chunks as big as a wine cork, put them in a jar, which you then fill with sherry, and keep if the fridge. Sherry and ginger are a great taste combination, so any time you need a bit of ginger, just fish out a lump, grate it or chop it, and use it immediately. If you feel a cold coming on, the jar is there for a quick remedy, or, to be more polite, you can put it in a glass and add a little whiskey.

Food without spices is like undeveloped film, waiting for something great to happen to it. Pasta is the ideal medium for free-style cooking, a blank screen on which you project flavours and colours and get immediate results. Remember the joys of finger-painting, or the book you always wanted to write? That's pasta.

Pasta with Sausage and Prawns

1	small onion	1
3	cloves garlic	3
2	tomatoes	2
2 tbsp	vegetable oil	25 mL
1	spicy Italian sausage	1
1	sweet red pepper	1
8	unshelled raw prawns	8
½ cup	red wine	125 mL
8 oz	uncooked pasta,	250 g
	like rigatoni or penne	
	A handful of parsley	
	Salt	
	Pepper	

Bring a large pot of water (for the pasta) to a boil while someone chops the onion, garlic and tomatoes. Heat the oil in a saucepan over medium-high heat, and add the chopped onion and garlic to it. Cook for 2–3 minutes, until the onion starts to turn clear. Add the tomatoes, and cook for a further 3 minutes. While you slice the sausage into bite-sized coins, have someone else chop the red pepper and rinse, peel and devein the prawns. Add the sausage and chopped pepper to the saucepan, cook it for 2 minutes and then add the wine. Reduce the heat to low, cover and let the mixture simmer for about 15 minutes. In the meantime, add the pasta to the large pot of boiling water, and cook it for 8–10 minutes, until it is tender. Stir the prawns into the sausage mixture, and cook for 2 minutes or until the prawns just turn pink. Meanwhile, have someone chop the parsley. Drain the pasta. Season the sauce with salt and pepper, and serve over the drained pasta, sprinkled with parsley.

LINGUINE WITH MINT AND PEAS

2	cloves garlic	2
	A couple of sprigs of mint	
	A handful of uncooked linguine	
2 tbsp	vegetable oil	25 mL
1 cup	fresh or frozen peas	250 mL
½ cup	whipping cream	125 mL
	Salt	
	Pepper	

*P*ut a large pot of water on to boil (for the pasta) while someone chops the garlic and mint. Cook the pasta until tender, about 10 minutes. In the meantime, make the sauce: heat the oil in a frypan over medium heat. Add the garlic and cook for 2 minutes, stirring so it doesn't burn. Add the peas and cream, and bring the mixture to a boil. Reduce the heat to low and let the mixture simmer until the peas are done, about 5 minutes. Drain the pasta. Stir in the mint, season with salt and pepper, and serve over the drained pasta.

QUICK AND SIMPLE TOMATO SAUCE

3 tbsp	vegetable oil	45 mL
1	small onion	1
3	cloves garlic	3
4	very ripe tomatoes	4
	(or 1 can of crushed tomatoes)	
	A few sprigs of basil	
1 tbsp	tomato paste	15 mL
⅓ cup	red wine	75 mL
½ tsp	salt	2 mL

Heat the oil in a large frypan over medium-high heat while someone chops the onion, garlic, tomatoes and basil. Add the onion and garlic to the frypan, and cook for 2–3 minutes, until the onion starts to turn clear. Add the tomatoes and tomato paste, and cook for 2 minutes. Add the wine, reduce the heat to low, cover and let the mixture simmer while you watch a movie or teach yourself how to knit: 30 minutes for a "loose" sauce, 45 minutes for an intensely flavoured, thicker sauce. You may need to check the sauce once in awhile to make sure there is still a little liquid in the pan (if not, just add some water or more wine). Season the sauce with the salt and basil, and serve over your favourite cooked pasta.

Pasta with Green Beans, Potatoes and Pesto

4 oz	green beans	100 g
1	clove garlic	1
2 tbsp	pine nuts or walnuts	25 mL
	A handful of basil leaves	
¼ cup	grated Parmesan cheese	50 mL
¼ cup	good olive oil	50 mL
	A handful of uncooked pasta, like spaghetti	
4 oz	nugget potatoes	100 g

*P*ut two pots of water on to boil: one for the pasta, and one for the beans and potatoes. While you wait for the water to boil, trim the green beans and have someone else make the pesto: Put the garlic, nuts, basil and cheese into a food processor, and blend until smooth. With the processor still running, drizzle the olive oil into the mixture, and blend until smooth again. When the water is ready, put the pasta in one pot, and cook until tender, about 10 minutes, depending on the type of pasta. In the other pot, cook the green beans for 3–4 minutes, remove them from the water and run cold water over them until they are cool. Boil the potatoes in the same pot for about 5–6 minutes, until tender. Drain them and cut them into bite-sized pieces. Drain the pasta, and toss it with the potatoes, green beans and pesto.

A Simple Sicilian Spaghetti

	A handful of uncooked spaghetti	
	A handful of walnuts	
	A handful of parsley	
1 tbsp	butter	15 mL
	Salt	
	Pepper	
2 oz	blue cheese	50 g

Cook the spaghetti in a large pot of boiling water until tender, about 10 minutes. In the meantime, have someone chop the walnuts and parsley and set them aside. When the spaghetti is done, drain it and toss it with the butter. Season with salt and pepper. Crumble the blue cheese over top, and serve sprinkled with the walnuts and parsley.

Pasta Fagioli

Simple comfort.

2 tbsp	vegetable oil	25 mL
3	cloves garlic	3
1	large carrot	1
1	small onion	1
1	stalk celery	1
	A handful of basil	
1	tin (14 oz/398 mL) chickpeas	1
	or white (cannellini or navy) beans	
1 tsp	salt	5 mL
½ tsp	pepper	2 mL
	A handful of uncooked small pasta	
2 cups	chicken stock or water	500 mL
	Juice of 1 lemon	
	Grated Parmesan cheese	

While you heat the oil in a large saucepan over medium-high heat, have someone chop the garlic, carrot, onion, celery and basil. Open the tin of chickpeas, drain them and rinse them under cold water. Add all of the chopped vegetables and basil to the pan, as well as the salt and pepper. Cook for 3 minutes, and then add the chickpeas, pasta and stock. Bring to a boil, and reduce the heat to low. Simmer for 20 minutes or until the pasta is done and the soup is nice and thick. Add the lemon juice, stir and serve sprinkled with Parmesan cheese.

Penne with Tomatoes and Mushrooms

8 oz	uncooked penne	250 g
3	tomatoes	3
1	small onion	1
2	cloves garlic	2
½ lb	specialty mushrooms, such as	250 g
	oyster or portabello, or regular mushrooms	
	A handful of parsley	
2 tbsp	vegetable oil	25 mL
¼ cup	water	50 mL
	Salt	
	Pepper	

While you put the pasta on to cook, have someone chop the tomatoes, onion, garlic, mushrooms and parsley. Heat the oil in a frypan over medium-high heat. Add the tomatoes, onion and garlic, and cook for 3 minutes, stirring. Add the water and mushrooms, and cook for a further 10 minutes, until the tomatoes have collapsed. Meanwhile, have someone drain the pasta. Season the sauce with salt and pepper. Serve the pasta with the sauce and a sprinkling of parsley on top.

CAULIFLOWER PASTA

1	small head cauliflower	1
8 oz	uncooked, small pasta	250 g
	(like macaroni or fusilli)	
2	cloves garlic	2
6	anchovies	6
	A handful of parsley	
2 tbsp	vegetable oil	25 mL
½ tsp	pepper	2 mL
	A pinch of red pepper flakes	

*P*ut a big pot of water on to boil while someone cuts the cauliflower into small florets. When the water is ready, add the pasta and the cauliflower, and cook for 10 minutes, until they are both tender. In the meantime, chop the garlic, anchovies and parsley. When the pasta and cauliflower are done, drain and toss with the oil, garlic, anchovies, pepper, red pepper flakes and parsley. Eat immediately.

Fettuccine with Spinach, Zucchini and Walnuts

8 oz	uncooked fettuccine	250 g
1	small onion	1
2	cloves garlic	2
2	medium zucchini	2
1	bunch fresh spinach	1
2 tbsp	vegetable oil	25 mL
	Salt	
	Pepper	
	A handful of walnuts	
4 oz	provolone or	100 g
	Monterey Jack cheese	

Put the pasta on to cook while someone chops the onion, garlic and zucchini. Wash the spinach, cut the stems off and set it aside. While the pasta cooks, heat the oil in a frypan over medium-high heat. Add the onion, garlic and zucchini. Cook for 4–5 minutes, stirring, until the zucchini starts to turn clear. Add the spinach, cover and let the mixture cook for another 2 minutes. Remove the lid, season with salt and pepper, and cook for another 2 minutes, until the water from the spinach evaporates. In the meantime, have someone chop the walnuts and grate the cheese. When the pasta is done, drain it and toss it with the spinach mixture. Serve sprinkled with the chopped walnuts and grated provolone.

MACARONI AND CHEESE

8 oz	uncooked macaroni	250 g
2 tbsp	butter	25 mL
2 tbsp	flour	25 mL
2 cups	milk	500 mL
2 cups	grated cheddar	500 mL
	or Monterey Jack cheese	
½ tsp	dry mustard	2 mL
	A pinch of paprika	

Preheat your oven to 350°F (180°C). Put the macaroni on to cook, and in the meantime, make the cheese sauce. Melt the butter in the saucepan over medium heat. Stir in the flour to make a paste, and cook for a few minutes to get rid of the raw flour taste. Remove the pan from the heat. Stir in the milk, a bit at a time, so it doesn't get lumpy. Return the pan to the heat, and keep stirring until the mixture comes to a boil and starts to thicken. While you are doing that, have someone grease a baking dish large enough to hold the pasta. Stir the grated cheese, mustard and paprika into the milk mixture, reduce the heat to low and keep stirring until the cheese has melted. Remove the sauce from the heat. When the macaroni is cooked, drain it and place it in the greased baking dish. Pour the sauce over top and bake, uncovered, for 20–25 minutes, until bubbly and lightly browned.

SPAGHETTINI WITH CLAMS, BURNT BUTTER AND LEMON

1 lb	small fresh clams in the shell	500 g
½	medium onion	½
	A handful of parsley	
2 tbsp	butter	25 mL
½ cup	white wine	125 mL
1 tbsp	fresh lemon juice	15 mL
1	tin (5 oz/142 g) clams	1
	A handful of uncooked spaghettini	
2 tbsp	grated Parmesan cheese	25 mL

While one of you puts 4 quarts of cold, salted water on to boil, the other can clean the clams by brushing the shells under cold running water. Discard any that are not tightly closed. While you finely chop the onion and parsley, get someone to heat the butter in a pan over high heat until it begins to brown. Reduce the heat to low, add onions and cook until they are soft. Add the fresh clams, wine, lemon juice and the juice from the canned clams and bring to a boil. Cover and reduce to a simmer for about 5 minutes. Discard any that do not open. Have someone put the pasta in the boiling water while you add the canned clams and parsley to the sauce. Keep the sauce warm over low heat until the pasta is cooked. Cook the pasta until it is tender but yields to the bite, drain and toss in the sauce. Serve immediately with Parmesan cheese on the side. This dish is still tremendous without the fresh clams — just reduce the wine, lemon juice and juice from the canned clams by one-third by simmering for about 10 minutes before adding the canned clams.

VEGETABLES

*E*ating vegetables doesn't mean you have to be a Buddhist or wear Birkenstocks winter and summer and look like a pink-eyed rabbit. Everybody's eating more vegetables today, and because of that a lot more people are learning to cook. Any fool can burn a steak, but vegetables need care, a little gentling, a little understanding. The sad thing is, nobody in the supermarkets seems to know anything about them. You ask, and they don't know ("I guess you boil it . . ."). Yet day after day there are more exotics appearing on the shelves. You can see people looking at something simple like an artichoke, or even asparagus, and there's nobody there to help them. They worry, they dither, they put it back on the shelf and they go right back to the iceberg lettuce. We're eating a lot less meat and a little more fish, and there are more and more roadside stands selling vegetables, so obviously there's a market for green leaves.

You can spend hours in a bookshop looking at the shelves of fancy and specialized vegetable cookbooks. *Jane Grigson's Vegetable Book* by Penguin is probably the most comprehensive, the most straightforward and probably also the cheapest, and any good Italian book will have more good vegetable recipes than you can imagine. But the real secret to cooking vegetables, hot or cold, is a decent vinaigrette. Which means good olive oil and good vinegar, and also means you'll never again buy bottled salad dressings from the store.

On salads, on hot vegetables, even on lukewarm vegetables, a vinaigrette is the best thing that ever happened in your kitchen. You can read all kinds of stuff about vinaigrettes — how to whisk and fold and blend and stir — until it all sounds like an advertisement for a massage parlour. While the truth is that all you need is a jar. One of those small spice jars is fine. And then remember that you don't need as much vinegar as they say. Wine vinegar's okay. So's cider vinegar. But malt's not — that's for fish and chips. It's the oil you want to taste, the oil making a soft gentle base for the vegetables or the herbs and spices you put in the dressing.

So. Pour at most half an inch of vinegar into the jar. You can see it easily from the side. Now pour in the oil, slowly, and you'll see it float on top of the vinegar. Keep pouring until you've got five times as much oil as vinegar. Add half a teaspoon of salt, the same of ground pepper, about a teaspoon of mustard and just a pinch of sugar. Screw on the lid, give it a vigorous shake and it'll be blended and smooth.

This is the base. You make it, you use some of it and the rest you keep in the fridge. It's the base, and you can add whatever you like to it each time you use it. Some finely chopped parsley, or chives (whatever herb you fancy), some chopped garlic, some sesame seeds — you choose. If you want an egg-based vinaigrette, almost a Greek dressing, put an egg yolk in the jar with the vinaigrette, screw on the lid (don't forget that) and then give it another good shake. It will blend into a smooth sauce that is great with asparagus, or on sliced tomatoes, even tossed with spinach.

If you want to make a fancy vinaigrette, use lemon juice instead of vinegar, or grapefruit juice, or even orange juice.

Chop an anchovy fine, add that to the jar with a clove of garlic chopped fine and you've got an instant Caesar salad. And if you need to astonish both of you, pour it over freshly cooked asparagus.

The oldest man in the world, at least the oldest man we know about, is in China. He's 131, he has no bad habits, like alcohol or tobacco, and he also has no teeth. Most of all, he has no love life, which seems quite understandable at 131, but he's very keen on pointing out that he never has had one. The reason for his longevity is the bachelor lifestyle, he says, and he eats only vegetables. So he sits in the corner drinking tea, sucking down cabbage soup, and his only pleasure seems to be in telling everybody he meets that he's 131, next year he'll be 132 and the year after. . .

Which doesn't sound like a whole lot of fun. I know a few people like that, none of them 131, but they might just as well be — they live their lives in a state of constant and solitary virtue. I got stuck with one a couple of months ago. This one was a vegetarian, and she spent most of the first half hour at supper telling everybody at the table about the poor lambs and the poor cows and the poor chickens. She'd brought her own tofu wieners and a bunch or organic greens. There's nothing wrong with that — you eat what you like and not what I like — but she sat there chewing away (25 times each mouthful) on those perfectly dreadful rice cakes, the ones that look and taste like Styrofoam, and she just couldn't stop sermonizing.

Mr. Chan, the 131-year-old Chinese man, thinks he'll go on forever, and I thought she was going to go on forever too, talking about how good, kind, considerate and perfect she was. She seemed to have a vision of an afterlife, her own kind of heaven, which was a great big green field filled with animals and people and kids, all of them being very happy eating rice cakes.

But she didn't like cats, particularly my cat, which is a nice ordinary cat that sits on laps and purrs. She was having a hard time explaining how she'd make sure that there weren't any cats in heaven. But most of all she was being virtuous, as in "I'm perfect and you aren't," and the more things she could tell us she didn't do, the more virtuous she felt.

Finally somebody at the table (a friend who has his share of vices, one of which is a liking for red wine) decided that she was a bore and that he wasn't getting much pleasure out of *not* telling her. So he did, and it turned into a full-scale battle. She got mad and he got mad, and they both started to behave like an old married couple — "You did . . ." "I didn't . . ." "You did . . ." "I didn't . . ."

There's no immediately happy ending to this. They didn't suddenly discover one another and settle down to a life of shared bliss with meat on Monday and tofu on Tuesday. They did go out on a date, and they fought all over again. They had a terrible time, and they still say they can't stand one another. But they go out regularly — he drinks, she eats tofu wieners — but they've discovered they both like tomato salad, fried green beans, cabbage and radishes. They can't stop being pig-headed, they still lecture one another and they squabble. Neither of them is quite so virtuous, and it would be nice (and convenient) if I could say that vegetables had brought them together.

I think it's lust — not pure lust but lust well spiced with tolerance. The vegetables were just a part of it. It's what you do, not what you don't do, that matters.

TURKISH GREEN BEANS

8 oz	green beans	250 g
½ cup	walnuts	125 mL
¾ cup	bread crumbs	175 mL
1	clove garlic	1
	Juice of 1 lemon	
	A handful of parsley	
½ tsp	salt	2 mL
	A pinch of pepper	
⅓ cup	olive oil	75 mL

*P*ut a pot of water on to boil. While you trim the stem end of the green beans, have someone start making the sauce: place the walnuts, bread crumbs, garlic, lemon juice, parsley, salt and pepper in a food processor, and blend to a paste. Add the olive oil while the machine is still running, and whiz until everything is smooth. Cook the green beans in the boiling water until tender but still bright green, about 4 minutes. Drain the beans, spoon the sauce over top and serve.

Broccoli with Feta and Mint

2 tbsp	vegetable oil	25 mL
8 oz	broccoli (about 2 heads)	250 g
1	clove garlic	1
	A few sprigs of mint	
	Salt	
	Pepper	
½ cup	feta cheese	50 mL

Heat the oil in a frypan over medium-high heat while someone chops the broccoli into bite-sized pieces. Add the broccoli to the pan, and cook for 1 minute. While it is cooking, have someone finely chop the garlic and mint leaves. Add the garlic to the pan, and cook for 3 minutes. Season with salt and pepper, sprinkle with the mint leaves and crumble the feta over top.

German Onion Tart

4 oz	side bacon	100 g
1	large onion	1
1	unbaked 9-inch (23 cm) pie shell	1
1 cup	light cream	250 mL
2	eggs	2
	A pinch of nutmeg	
	A pinch of salt	
½ tsp	pepper	2 mL

*P*reheat your oven to 375°F (190°C) and heat a dry frypan on your stove over medium-high heat. Cut the bacon into small pieces while someone else thinly slices the onion. Add the bacon to the frypan, and cook until crisp, about 6 minutes. Remove the bacon from the pan (but leave the fat in), and spread the bacon over the bottom of the pie shell. Add the onions to the frypan, and reduce the heat to medium. Cook until soft and caramelized, about 20 minutes. While the onions are cooking, have someone beat the cream, eggs, nutmeg, salt and pepper together until well blended. Place the caramelized onions in the pie shell, and pour the egg mixture over top. Bake for 25–30 minutes, until the eggs have set. Remove the tart from the oven, let it cool for a couple of minutes before slicing and serve.

...ᴄʜ Fʀɪᴇs

2	sweet potatoes or yams	2
	Vegetable oil	
	Cayenne	
	Salt	
	Pepper	

*P*reheat your oven to 400°F (200°C). Cut the sweet potatoes into small wedges, and place them in a greased baking dish or on a greased baking sheet. Drizzle the wedges with oil, sprinkle with cayenne, salt and pepper, and bake, uncovered, for 25–30 minutes or until crispy on the outside, tender on the inside.

Sᴘɪᴄʏ Nᴜɢɢᴇᴛ Pᴏᴛᴀᴛᴏᴇs

1 lb	nugget potatoes	450 g
2 tbsp	vegetable oil	25 mL
½ tsp	red pepper flakes	2 mL
	Salt	
	Pepper	

*P*reheat your oven to 400°F (205°C). Cut the potatoes into halves or quarters. Pour the oil onto a baking sheet, and roll the nugget potatoes in the oil until they are well coated. Sprinkle with the red pepper flakes, salt and pepper, and bake, uncovered, for 20–25 minutes, until the potatoes are done.

Pan Haggerty

A coal miner's supper from northeast England.	3 tbsp	vegetable oil	45 mL
	3	small potatoes	3
	1	small onion	1
	¼ lb	cheddar cheese	100 g

Heat the oil in a frypan over medium-high heat. While you thinly slice the potatoes and onion, have someone else grate the cheese. Reduce the heat to low, lay one-third of the potato slices in the bottom of the pan and lay one-third of the onion slices on top of that. Sprinkle with half of the grated cheese. Top with another layer of potatoes and another layer of onions. Sprinkle the rest of the cheese on top. Cover with the remaining onions and finally with the rest of the potatoes. Cover and cook for 20–25 minutes. Remove the lid, and invert a plate over the frypan. Flip the frypan over so that the potato mixture winds up on the plate, cooked side up. Add a bit more oil to the pan, and slide the potatoes back into the pan to cook the other side. Cook for 10 minutes, covered, and then serve.

Zucchini Pie

1	large zucchini	1
1	unbaked 9-inch (23 cm) pie shell	1
8 oz	feta cheese	250 g
	A pinch of nutmeg	
2	eggs	2
¼ cup	milk	50 mL
⅓ cup	cornmeal	75 mL
½ tsp	pepper	2 mL
	A pinch of dried oregano	

*P*reheat your oven to 375°F (190°C). Slice the zucchini into very thin pieces, and place them in the bottom of the pie shell. Crumble the feta cheese over top. Meanwhile, have someone beat the remaining ingredients into a thick batter and pour it over the zucchini and feta. Bake, uncovered, for 35–40 minutes, until puffed up and browned on top. Serve hot or cold.

Broccoli with Sausage and White Beans

8 oz	broccoli	250 g
1	small onion	1
2	tomatoes	2
	A handful of parsley	
	A sprig of rosemary	
2 tbsp	vegetable oil	25 mL
2	mild Italian sausages	2
1	tin (14 oz/398 mL)	1
	white (cannellini or navy) beans	
½ cup	water	125 mL
	Salt	
	Pepper	

Chop the broccoli, onion, tomatoes, parsley and rosemary while someone else heats the oil in a frypan over medium-high heat. Slice the sausages into ½-inch (1 cm) thick coins, and add them to the frypan. Cook for 3–4 minutes, turning them as they brown. While they cook, have someone open the tin of white beans, drain them and rinse them under cold water. Shove the sausages to one side of the frypan, and add the onion and tomatoes. Cook for another 3 minutes, and then add the broccoli, beans, rosemary and water. Cover and cook for 5 minutes. Season with salt and pepper, and serve with the parsley sprinkled over top.

A Lovely Zucchini Sauté

2	medium zucchinis,	2
	one green and one yellow	
2	cloves garlic	2
	A sprig of basil	
3 tbsp	good olive oil	45 mL
	Zest of 1 lemon	
	Salt	
	Pepper	

Dice the zucchini and chop the garlic and basil while someone heats the oil in a frypan over medium-high heat. Add the zucchini to the pan, and let it cook for 4–5 minutes. Add the garlic, basil and lemon zest. Cook for another 2–3 minutes, stirring. Season with salt and pepper, and serve.

Spinach with Pine Nuts and Raisins

1	bunch fresh spinach	1
2 tbsp	vegetable oil	25 mL
	A handful of raisins	
	A handful of pine nuts	
	Salt	
	Pepper	
	A splash of balsamic vinegar	

Cut the stems off the spinach, and discard them. Wash the spinach thoroughly while someone heats the oil in a frypan over medium-high heat. Add the spinach to the pan, stir well, cover and let cook for 2 minutes. Remove the lid, stir in the raisins and pine nuts, and cook for another minute or so. Season with salt and pepper, and serve with a bit of balsamic vinegar drizzled over top.

LEEKS WITH WALNUTS AND GINGER

1	leek	1
	A handful of walnuts	
2 tbsp	butter	25 mL
1 inch	fresh ginger	2.5 cm
	Salt	

Have someone cut the leek in half lengthwise and rinse out all of the mud that's stuck between the leaves. Meanwhile, toast the walnuts in a dry frypan over medium-high heat. Remove them from the pan, and set them aside. Heat the butter in the same frypan over medium heat, and have someone chop the leek and grate the ginger. Add the leeks and ginger to the pan, and cook for 8–10 minutes, stirring, until the leeks are softened and bright green. Toss with the walnuts, season with salt and serve.

Cabbage and Butter

Cheap, simple, lovely.

½	head cabbage	½
2 tbsp	butter	25 mL
	Salt	
	Pepper	
	A pinch of nutmeg	

Slice the cabbage into thin pieces while someone melts the butter in a frypan over medium heat. Add the cabbage to the pan, cover and cook for 4–5 minutes. Remove the lid, and cook, stirring, for a further 3–4 minutes, until the cabbage is wilted and is starting to brown. Season with salt, pepper and nutmeg, and serve.

CAULIFLOWER CHEESE

1	small head cauliflower	1
2 tbsp	butter	25 mL
1 ¼ tsp	flour	7 mL
1 cup	milk	250 mL
4 oz	cheddar or Monterey Jack cheese	125 g
½ tsp	salt	2 mL
	A pinch of cayenne	
	A pinch of nutmeg	
¼ cup	bread crumbs	50 mL

Preheat your oven to 400°F (200°C). Have someone chop the cauliflower into small florets and put them on to cook in a large pot of water. In the meantime, make the cheese sauce: Melt the butter in a saucepan over medium heat, and add the flour, stirring to make a paste. Cook for a few minutes to get rid of the raw flour taste. Remove the pan from the heat, and stir the milk in slowly so no lumps form. Return the pan to the heat, and cook the mixture until it comes to a boil and starts to thicken. Have someone grate the cheese. Stir the salt, cayenne, nutmeg and grated cheese into the milk mixture. Stir until the cheese has melted, and remove the pan from the heat. Drain the cauliflower, and place it in an ungreased baking dish. Smother the cauliflower with the cheese sauce, sprinkle it with bread crumbs and bake, uncovered, for 15–20 minutes, until nice and bubbly.

ASPARAGUS WITH LIGHTLY CURRIED YOGURT

1	bunch asparagus	1
1 cup	yogurt	250 mL
2 tsp	curry powder	10 mL

*P*ut a large pot of water on to boil. Hold the asparagus horizontally in your hands, and snap the stalks off (the stalks will naturally break where the asparagus gets woody). Discard the ends. When the water is ready, add the asparagus tips, and cook for 3 minutes, until the asparagus is cooked and still bright green. While the asparagus is cooking, have someone mix together the yogurt and curry powder, and set it aside. Drain the asparagus, and run it under cold water. Pat dry and serve with the yogurt mixture spooned over top.

Fried Okra

4 oz	okra	100 g	
¼ cup	cornmeal	50 mL	
½ tsp	paprika	2 mL	
¼ tsp	salt	1 mL	
	A pinch of cayenne		
1	egg	1	
½ tsp	Dijon mustard	2 mL	
3 tbsp	vegetable oil	45 mL	

While you cut the okra into ¼-inch (5 mm) rounds, have someone mix together the cornmeal, paprika, salt and cayenne. In a separate bowl, combine the egg and Dijon mustard. Dip the okra first in the egg mixture and then in the cornmeal mixture. Heat the vegetable oil over high heat until it begins to smoke, and then carefully toss in the coated okra. Fry until golden brown on all sides, about 2 minutes. Transfer to a paper towel-lined dish to absorb any excess oil.

Rice, Other Grains
and Beans

Rice used to be thrown at weddings to ensure fertility — lots of little grains meant lots of little babies. But throwing rice isn't fashionable any more — in fact throwing anything is frowned upon. The churches don't want to clean up, and with all those people out there starving for a bowl of rice, nobody's going to feel very good about wasting it on a bride who may not be thinking about fertility at all.

Rice still hasn't moved into our Western consciousness as a regular staple, rather than as an occasional and unusual treat or a necessity with Chinese food. We make paella, and restaurants serve rice as an alternative to the usual baked, boiled or fried potato. It seems that many grandmas have secret recipes for rice pudding, but that's about as far as it goes — perhaps some Rice Krispies and a bit of rice bran for the health food devotees.

I discovered rice the first time I was in Japan. I went for five days and ended up staying for three months. I didn't have much money, and I ate in small Japanese restaurants or with Japanese families. Which meant getting used to a lot of rice. We had rice for breakfast, yesterday's rice, with dried seaweed sprinkled on top, some smoked fish, some pickled radish, a raw egg and a bowl of soup. It's surprising how soon you get used to it, and get to need it. I'd have a couple of bowls of rice for lunch with a bit of fish, and by the time I left I was up to three bowls at supper.

I ate sometimes with wealthy people and sometimes with people who were well down on the economic scale, but they all approached their rice with the same enthusiasm. It was almost religious. They would almost smile at it as they first took the bowl in their hands, and then they'd chew on the first mouthful with the same sort of concentration as you see on the faces of wine tasters, and they'd nod, almost everybody at the table would nod, like football players in a huddle, and then everybody would get down to the serious business of eating.

The rice was never mucked about with. Nobody poured soy sauce on it. It was kept pure and simple, and after a mouthful of tempura or barbecued fish or a bit of pork, everybody took a mouthful of rice and enjoyed the flavour of that. They explained it to me as being the same as black and white photography: the simple, bland nature of the rice contrasted with the complicated flavours of the cooked food — each needs the  other to be fully appreciated. "You couldn't see the black if it weren't for the white," said the man who explained it to me. When we'd finished, particularly after big meals in the country, meals after kite festivals or special occasion meals, people would frequently take their rice bowl, and as a last thing they would put a spoonful or two of rice in it, pour tea over the top, stir it around and slurp it up. "To remember," they said, "to remember the hard times, when there was nothing to eat but rice and tea."

Even today, when I eat rice, I always feel vaguely holy — each grain, separate and complete, is like a small Buddhist prayer. Rice isn't hard times to me — it's good times and shared times.

Spicy Chickpeas with Tomatoes and Lime

1	tin (14 oz/398 mL) chickpeas	1
2	tomatoes	2
1	small onion	1
1	clove garlic	1
½ inch	fresh ginger	1 cm
2	small green chili peppers	2
2 tbsp	vegetable oil	25 mL
	Juice of 2 limes	
	A handful of cilantro	
	Salt	
	Pepper	

While you open the tin of chickpeas and rinse them under cold water, have someone start chopping the tomatoes, onion, garlic, ginger and chili peppers. Heat the oil in a saucepan over medium-high heat. Add the chopped tomatoes, onion and garlic, and cook, stirring, for 3–4 minutes, until the tomatoes start to collapse. Add the ginger and chili peppers, and cook for another 2 minutes. Stir in the drained chickpeas, and squeeze the lime juice over top. Stir, and let the whole mixture cook for a further 3 minutes. In the meantime, chop a bit of cilantro. Season with salt and pepper, and serve with the chopped cilantro sprinkled over top.

Lemon Rice

1	small onion	1
1	lemon	1
2 tbsp	butter	25 mL
⅔ cup	uncooked long-grain rice	150 mL
1 ⅓ cups	chicken stock or water	325 mL
	Salt	
	Pepper	

Preheat your oven to 400°F (205°C). While you chop the onion, have someone grate the zest of half a lemon (leave the lemon whole — that way you won't get juice all over your hands). Melt the butter in an ovenproof saucepan over medium heat. Add the chopped onion and lemon zest, and cook for 2–3 minutes. Add the rice, and cook for a further 2 minutes, stirring constantly. The rice should be translucent and have absorbed all of the butter. Stir in the stock, and bring the mixture to a boil. Cover the saucepan, and put it in the oven. Bake it for 25 minutes, until all of the stock has been absorbed. Season with salt and pepper, and serve.

DAL

A staple of East
Indian cooking.

1 cup	dried red lentils	250 mL
2 cups	water	500 mL
2 tbsp	vegetable oil	25 mL
1	small onion	1
2	cloves garlic	2
1	tomato	1
½ inch	fresh ginger	1 cm
½ tsp	turmeric	2 mL
	A pinch of cinnamon	
½ tsp	salt	2 mL

Place the lentils and water in a pot, bring to a boil and cook over medium heat for about 20 minutes or until the lentils are tender and most of the water has been absorbed. While the lentils are cooking, heat the oil in a frypan over medium-high heat. Have someone chop the onion, garlic, tomato and ginger. Add the onion and garlic to the pan, and cook for 2–3 minutes. Add the tomato, ginger and spices, and reduce the heat to medium. Cook for 12 minutes or until the tomato starts to collapse. When the lentils are done, add them and any liquid still left to the frypan. Toss, season with salt and serve. Great with flatbread, tortillas or pita.

Baked Polenta

1 ⅓ cups	water	375 mL
½ tsp	salt	2 mL
½ cup	cornmeal	125 mL
1 tsp	butter	5 mL
2 oz	blue or Gorgonzola cheese	50 mL

Preheat your oven to 350°F (180°C). Place the water and salt into a pot, and whisk in the cornmeal, making sure there are no lumps. Bring the mixture to a boil over medium heat, stirring. Cook for 2–3 minutes, until the mixture is quite thick. Add the butter, and pour the mixture into a greased baking dish. Crumble the cheese over top, and bake, uncovered, for 20 minutes or until the cheese has completely melted and is starting to brown. Terrific hot or cold.

FAGIOLI TOSCANA

Beans	2 tbsp	good olive oil	25 mL
Tuscan style.	1	tin (19 oz/540 mL white (cannellini or navy) beans	1
	2	cloves garlic	2
	2	fresh sage leaves	2
	¼ cup	water	50 mL
		Salt	
		Pepper	

While you heat the oil in a frypan over medium heat, have someone open the tin of beans, drain them and rinse them in cold water. Chop the garlic, add it to the oil and cook gently, making sure it doesn't burn. Add the beans, sage and water, and heat through. Season with salt and pepper, and serve.

Note: This also makes a nice dip. Place all of the ingredients in a food processor (no need to cook anything), and whiz until smooth.

Moroccan Chickpeas and Couscous

2 cups	water	500 mL
1 cup	couscous	250 mL
2 tbsp	vegetable oil	25 mL
1	tin (14 oz/398 mL) chickpeas	1
1	small onion	1
1	clove garlic	1
2	tomatoes	2
½ inch	fresh ginger	1 cm
	A handful of cilantro	
	A pinch of saffron	
	A pinch of turmeric	
⅛ tsp	cayenne	1 mL
⅛ tsp	cinnamon	1 mL
½ tsp	salt	2 mL

Bring the water to a boil in a small saucepan over high heat. Stir in the couscous, cover and turn the heat off. While you heat the oil in a fry-pan over medium-high heat, have someone open the tin of chickpeas, drain them and rinse them under cold water. Chop the onion, garlic, tomatoes, ginger and cilantro. Add the onion and garlic to the pan, and cook for 2–3 minutes. Reduce the heat to medium. Add the tomatoes, ginger, spices and salt, and cook for a further 8 minutes, stirring. Stir in the chickpeas, heat through and serve over the couscous, sprinkled with the chopped cilantro.

Quick Lentils

2 tbsp	vegetable oil	25 mL
1	tin (19 oz/540 mL) brown lentils	1
1	large carrot	1
2	cloves garlic	2
1	tomato	1
	A pinch of ground cloves	
	Salt	

*W*hile you heat the oil in a frypan over medium-high heat, have someone drain the lentils and rinse them under cold water. Chop the carrot, garlic and tomato, and add it to the pan. Cook for 4–5 minutes, and then add the lentils, cloves, and salt to taste. Heat through and serve.

Rice with Orange Zest and Green Onions

3 cups	chicken stock or water	750 mL
1	orange	1
2	green onions	2
1 ½ cups	uncooked long-grain rice	375 mL

*P*ut the stock on to boil while someone else zests the orange and finely chops the green onions. When the water boils, add the rice, orange zest and green onions, bring to a boil again and reduce the heat to low. Cover and simmer for 20 minutes or until all of the water has been absorbed by the rice.

Coconut Rice

⅜ cup	parboiled long-grain rice	175 mL
½ cup	coconut milk	125 mL
1 cup	cold water	250 mL
1	clove garlic	1
2	green onions	1
½ inch	fresh ginger	1 cm
	A few sprigs of thyme	
¼ tsp	salt	1 mL

While one of you washes the rice in cold water to remove some of the starch, the other can put the coconut milk in a pot with the cold water and bring it to a boil. Peel the garlic clove, and smash it flat with the broad side of your knife. Cut the green onions into three lengths, and smash them as well. Cut ginger into two slices, large enough to be easily spotted and removed when the rice is finished. Remove the thyme leaves from the stalks, and stir all of the ingredients into the boiling coconut milk. When the rice returns to the boil, reduce the heat, cover and let simmer for 15 minutes or until the liquid has all been absorbed. Discard the garlic and ginger, and serve.

FISH AND SEAFOOD

*F*ish is quick and easy: from start to finish you can have dinner on the table in 20 minutes. There are really only two things you need to know about fish. The first is to buy it fresh (if there's the slightest fishy smell about it, then forget it — just smile, say "no, thank you" and walk away). The second is not to overcook it. A minute too long in the pan, and the best fish can taste like cardboard. No matter how you cook it — bake, fry or poach — fish needs between 8 and 9 minutes per inch of thickness, measured at the thickest part. When it comes out of the pan, it continues to cook with its own heat for 2 or 3 minutes. Good fresh fish doesn't smell while it's cooking, and best of all it doesn't need a lot of fancy ingredients. Add a little butter or some good olive oil, a little salt and pepper, and the cheapest piece of fish will come alive for your tastebuds. If you do feel extravagant, a little saffron and a splash of cream will turn your 15-minute dinner into the hautest of cuisine, and a fancy little 1-minute salsa (2 spoonfuls of chutney stirred with 2 spoonfuls of white wine) will make it look bright enough for the centrefold of any gourmet magazine.

Fresh fish is best, but if you can't find it, then there's always frozen. Once again it has to *look* fresh, and even if you can't see the actual fish, the packet will tell you a lot. Bent-up corners, leaks or stains of any kind mean it's probably been badly kept, and it will be a disappointment — so don't buy it. Frozen fish is best in stews and soups, and it doesn't need to be defrosted. Just cut it into chunks, and put it in the pot for 10 minutes before serving. And finally, canned fish shouldn't be the last resort of the desperate. Sardines make great sandwiches with a little mayonnaise and some thinly sliced green onions, sockeye salmon makes wonderful fishcakes (and even a quick stir-fry), canned tuna takes on a whole new dimension with a couple of hard-boiled eggs and some black olives, and canned clams work well in chowder with a little extra garlic. Astronauts don't carry can openers, but any two earthbound people setting up house should make sure they have a little stock of canned fish.

SICILIAN PRAWNS AND BEANS

1	tin (14 oz/398 mL) white (cannellini or navy) beans	1
12	unshelled raw prawns	12
1	bay leaf	1
1 cup	chicken stock	250 mL
½ tsp	red pepper flakes	2 mL
½ tsp	salt	2 mL
1 tsp	pepper	5 mL
2	cloves garlic	2
	A handful of parsley	
2 tbsp	olive oil	25 mL
1	lemon	1

Drain and rinse the beans under cold running water. While someone rinses, peels and deveins the prawns, combine the beans, bay leaf, stock, red pepper flakes, salt and pepper in a saucepan, and bring this mixture to a boil. Reduce the heat to medium low, and let the mixture cook while you cook the prawns. Chop the garlic and parsley while you heat the oil in a frypan over high heat. Add the prawns and chopped garlic, and cook for 2 minutes, until the prawns just turn pink. While someone discards the bay leaf and divvies up the beans onto a couple of plates, cut the lemon in half and squeeze the juice over the prawns. Sprinkle them with parsley, and serve over the warm beans.

SALMON AND CORN CHOWDER

2 tbsp	butter	25 mL
1	leek	1
1	small potato	1
1	tin (6 ½ oz/184 g) canned salmon	1
1	tin (14 oz/398 mL) corn	1
	Juice of 1 lemon	
3 cups	fish stock or water	750 mL
1 cup	whipping cream	250 mL
	A couple of sprigs of dill	

Melt the butter in a large saucepan over medium heat while someone cuts the leek in half and rinses it. Chop the leek fine, and chop the potato into bite-sized pieces. Add the leek to the saucepan, and while it is cooking, have someone open the tins of salmon and corn and drain them. Add the drained salmon and corn to the saucepan, as well as the potato and lemon juice. Let the mixture cook for a minute, and then add the stock. Bring it all to a boil, and let it cook for 5–6 minutes, until the potatoes are tender. Stir in the whipping cream, and bring the soup to a boil again while you chop the dill. Serve the chowder with the dill sprinkled over top.

Fishcakes

2 tbsp	butter, melted	25 mL
1 cup	cold mashed potatoes	250 mL
1 tsp	fennel seeds	5 mL
1 tsp	pepper	5 mL
½	lemon	½
1	tin (6 ½ oz/184 g) sockeye salmon	1
	A few sprigs of parsley	
2 tbsp	vegetable oil	25 mL
1 cup	flour	250 mL

While you mash the butter into the potatoes, have someone crush the fennel seeds to release their flavour. Stir the fennel and pepper into the potatoes, and then grate the peel of the half of the lemon into the mixture. Squeeze in the lemon juice while someone opens the tin of salmon and drains it. Chop the parsley fine, and fold it into the potatoes with the drained salmon. While someone heats the oil in a frypan over medium-high heat, you can sprinkle your countertop with some of the flour. Take turns scooping out handfuls of the batter onto the countertop, and patting them into 1-inch (2.5 cm) thick cakes. Fry the cakes in the oil for about 3 minutes on each side or until lightly browned. Serve with salsa, chutney or just plain ketchup.

Sweet and Sour Salmon

2 tbsp	vegetable oil	25 mL
2	salmon fillets, about ½ lb/225 g each	2
1 tbsp	brown sugar	15 mL
1 tbsp	wine vinegar	15 mL
2 tbsp	red wine or apple juice	25 mL
1 tsp	grated lemon rind	5 mL
¼ tsp	red hot pepper flakes	1 mL
1 tsp	cornstarch	5 mL

Heat the oil in a frypan over medium-high heat. Add the salmon, skin side down, and while it is cooking, have someone combine the remaining ingredients in a small bowl, stirring them until everything is smooth and dissolved. Cook the salmon for 3 minutes, and then pour the marinade into the pan. Cook for 3 minutes, turn the salmon fillets over once more and cook for 1 more minute. Serve immediately.

SALMON WITH GINGER AND ORANGES

2	salmon steaks	2
2 tbsp	butter, softened	25 mL
1 inch	fresh ginger	2.5 cm
1	orange	1

*P*reheat your oven to 400°F (200°C). Lay the salmon steaks in an ungreased baking dish, and dot with the butter. Grate the fresh ginger and the zest of the orange over top. Cut the orange in half, and squeeze the juice onto the salmon and into the baking dish. Bake, uncovered, for 7 minutes, and serve with the pan juices drizzled over the fish.

BUTTERED CRAB

1 tbsp	butter	15 mL
	A handful of parsley	
4 oz	fresh crab meat broken into	100 g
	chunk (use canned if you absolutely have to)	
	Juice of 1 lemon	
2 tsp	bread crumbs	10 mL
¼ tsp	pepper	1 mL
2–4	pieces of good bread	2–4

*W*hile you melt the butter in a frypan over medium heat, have someone chop the parsley. Add it to the frypan, along with the crab, lemon juice, bread crumbs and pepper. Let the mixture cook for about 3 minutes. Pile it all on top of the slices of bread (you can toast the bread if you want to), and enjoy.

Roasted Fish and Tomatoes

2	tomatoes	2
1	small onion	1
1	clove garlic	1
1	lemon	1
2 tbsp	vegetable oil	25 mL
	A sprig of thyme	
2	white fish fillets	2
	(sea bass is great, but pricey; snapper is also nice)	
	Salt	
	Pepper	

Preheat your oven to 400°F (200°C). While you are waiting for the oven to get hot, have someone chop the tomatoes, onions and garlic into large pieces, and grate the zest of the lemon. Place the vegetables in a greased baking dish, and sprinkle with the oil, thyme leaves and lemon zest. Bake, uncovered, for 20 minutes or until the tomatoes have collapsed. Lay the fish on top of the vegetables, and bake, uncovered, for a further 7–8 minutes. Season with salt and pepper, and serve with the tomato mixture spooned over the fish.

Mexican Fishwife Fish

Any leftovers make soup the next day.

2 tbsp	vegetable oil	25 mL
3	tomatoes	3
1	small onion	1
1	sweet green pepper	1
1	clove garlic	1
	Juice of 1 lemon	
1 lb	cod fillets	450 g
1	bay leaf	1
	A pinch of thyme	
¼ tsp	cayenne or chili powder	1 mL
2 tbsp	tomato paste	25 mL

While you heat the oil in a frypan over medium-high heat and chop the tomatoes, onion, green pepper and garlic, have someone squeeze the lemon juice over the cod and set it aside. Add the chopped vegetables to the frypan and cook for 2–3 minutes, stirring. Reduce the heat to low, add the bay leaf, thyme and cayenne. Cover and continue cooking for 20 minutes or so, until the tomatoes have collapsed (you should check it a couple of times to make sure the sauce doesn't get too dry). Add the tomato paste to the sauce, stir it in well and then add the fish. Cover and simmer for 5 minutes, and then take the cover off and simmer for 5 more minutes. Discard the bay leaf. Serve with rice.

FIFTEEN-MINUTE FRENCH FISH STEW

1 lb	white fish	450 g
2 tbsp	butter	25 mL
1	small onion	1
8 oz	mushrooms	250 g
2	anchovy fillets	2
1 oz	whisky	30 mL
½ cup	white wine	125 mL
½ tsp	dried thyme	2 mL
	A handful of parsley	
¼ cup	sour cream	50 mL

While someone cuts the white fish into bite-sized pieces, go ahead and melt the butter in a large saucepan over medium heat. Chop the onion, mushrooms and anchovies. Add the onions to the saucepan, and cook for 3–4 minutes. Then add the fish, mushrooms, whisky, anchovies, wine and thyme. Stir it all together, and reduce the heat to medium-low. Simmer for 6–7 minutes. While it cooks, chop the parsley. Stir in the sour cream and serve with the parsley sprinkled over top.

SLIGHTLY SPICY SCALLOPS

¼ cup	butter	50 mL
1	egg yolk	1
½ cup	whipping cream	125 mL
1 tsp	salt	5 mL
½ tsp	pepper	2 mL
8 oz	scallops	250 g
½ tsp	curry powder	2 mL
½ cup	white wine	125 mL

While someone melts the butter in a frypan over medium heat, mix together the egg yolk, half of the cream, salt and pepper, and set the mixture aside. Place the scallops in the frypan, and cook them gently for about 2 minutes. Remove the scallops from the pan, and set them aside. Sprinkle the curry powder in the same frypan, and add the wine. Bring to a boil, and stir in the remaining cream. Reduce the heat to low. Pour the egg mixture slowly into the pan while stirring quickly, so the egg doesn't curdle. Return the scallops to the pan, cook for 2 minutes and serve.

Greek-Style Prawns with Feta

¼ cup	olive oil	50 mL
2	green onions	2
1	clove garlic	1
1	sweet red pepper	1
	A sprig of oregano	
	A handful of parsley	
2	tomatoes	2
1 dozen	prawns	1 dozen
½ cup	white wine	125 mL
	A splash of milk	
	Salt	
	Pepper	
¼ cup	feta cheese	50 mL

While the oil heats in a saucepan over medium heat, chop the green onions, garlic, red pepper, oregano, parsley and tomatoes. Have someone rinse the prawns in cold water, peel and devein them, and set them aside. Add the green onions, garlic, red pepper, oregano and parsley to the saucepan, and cook for 5 minutes, until softened. Add the wine, tomatoes and milk, and cook for 20 minutes. Add the prawns and cook until they just turn pink, about 2 minutes. Season with salt and pepper, and serve over rice with the feta crumbled over top and more white wine.

FISH SHACK-STYLE PAN-FRIED COD

1	egg	1
	A splash of milk	
½ cup	flour	125 mL
	A pinch of paprika	
¼ tsp	salt	1 mL
¼ tsp	pepper	1 mL
2 tbsp	vegetable oil	25 mL
2	pieces cod	2
	A sprig of parsley	
1	lemon	1

While you beat together the egg and milk in one bowl, have someone else mix the flour, paprika, salt and pepper in another. As you heat the oil in a frypan over medium-high heat, dip the cod pieces into the egg mixture first, and then dredge them in the flour mixture. Add the cod to the frypan, and cook for 2–3 minutes on each side. While the fish cooks, chop the parsley, and get someone to cut the lemon into wedges for you. Sprinkle the parsley over the fish, and serve with the lemon wedges and some potatoes.

Spicy Baked Fish

1 tbsp	ground coriander	15 mL
1 tbsp	cayenne	15 mL
½ tsp	ground cumin	2 mL
	A large pinch of turmeric	
½ tsp	salt	2 mL
	Juice of 1 lime	
	Water	
2	large pieces of any fish	2
	(preferably a firm white fish, like snapper)	

While you preheat your oven to 400°F (200°C), mix the spices and salt together thoroughly. Stir in the lime juice and enough water to make a paste. Spread the paste over both sides of the fish, and let the fish marinate for half an hour or so. Place the fish in a greased baking dish or ovenproof frypan and bake, uncovered, in the oven for 6–8 minutes. (Or you can cook the fish on your stove over medium-high heat for 3–4 minutes on each side.)

Fish with Grapes

8 oz	white fish	250 g
8 oz	(or one big handful) grapes	250 g
2 tbsp	flour	25 mL
1 tsp	salt	5 mL
½ tsp	pepper	2 mL
2 tbsp	butter	25 mL
½ tsp	dried tarragon	2 mL
½ glass	white wine	125 mL
	A bit more salt	

Cut the fish into bite-sized pieces while someone plucks the grapes from their stems, washes them and sets them aside. Mix the flour, salt and pepper together in a bowl, and dredge the fish pieces in it. Melt the butter in a frypan over medium heat, and add the fish. Cook, stirring, until the fish starts to become opaque, about 2–3 minutes. Add the grapes, tarragon, wine and a pinch more salt. Partially cover the pan, pour yourselves a glass of wine and let it all cook for about 7 minutes. Serve over rice.

MUSSELS AND BEER

2 lb	cultured mussels	1 kg
1	small onion	1
1	sweet red pepper	1
2	cloves garlic	2
	A few sprigs of thyme	
1 tbsp	vegetable oil	15 mL
¾ cup	lager beer	175 mL
¼ tsp	salt	1 mL

Flip a coin to see who gets the job of cleaning the mussels. Whoever loses the toss can rinse the mussels under cold running water to remove any grit and pull out any beards (the stringy bits attached to some of the mussels). Discard any that are not tightly closed. The winner can peel and slice the onion, slice the red pepper, mince the garlic and chop the thyme. Heat the oil in a large pot over medium-high heat, and cook the onions and peppers until they are soft. Stir in the garlic and thyme, and cook lightly, for only a minute. Stir in the mussels, and pour the beer over top. Pour the rest of the beer into a cold glass to share. Add the salt to the pot, and cover. Bring to a boil, reduce the heat to a simmer and let the mussels steam for about 5 minutes. Discard any mussels that have not opened. Watch you don't overcook the mussels or they will be tough and leathery.

CHICKEN

"Cookin' lasts, kissin' don't." The Pennsylvania Dutch had it almost right with this proverb — it's just a little out of date. Kitchens in those days belonged to the women. Men and boys had other things to do, and when they came in from the fields or wherever else they did their things, supper was their first priority — it had to be on the table, it usually had to be hot and it had to be something familiar. Meat and potatoes were the order of the day, second helpings were expected, men didn't do dishes and they most certainly didn't cook. Kissin' came later — lights out and missionary position, market day tomorrow, time to go to sleep.

Cooking was a chore, like milking and haying and ploughing the back forty. The weather decided what people ate. Strawberries were in for a couple of weeks, green peas for a month, cabbage all winter and carrots most of the year, left in the ground all winter to get as big (and as tough) as fence posts. Jakob and Maria would be lucky to have one cookbook, let alone a dozen, and you can be sure they never once sat down to talk about what they might serve the Vanderzalms next Friday, and would some of that Argentine Cabernet be okay with the pork chops?

Of course they fought — all married couples fight — but they didn't make up while doing the dishes, sneaking up, dish towel in hand, for a quick snug. They lived together, but it was a separate togetherness. They didn't share a lot, and they lived more in duty than in pleasure. Things are different today: most couples work hard at their separate jobs, and they sigh and mourn the good old days (which weren't really that good at all). But a lot more people are cooking together than ever before, cooking for one another and with one another. And they're finding that it isn't hard work and that it gives them a lot more pleasure than just coming home, hopping in the sack for a quickie and taking off for fried chicken at the drive-through. Take some chicken home, and cook it yourself, and you might find that kissin' lasts longer with cookin'.

Pizzaiola

1 tbsp	vegetable oil	15 mL
4	chicken thighs	4
5	tomatoes	5
	(or a 19 oz/540 mL tin)	
4	cloves garlic	4
½ cup	white or red wine	125 mL
1 cup	chicken stock	250 mL
1 tsp	dried oregano	5 mL
	Salt	
	Lots of pepper	

Heat the oil in a frypan over medium-high heat. Add the chicken, skin side down, and get someone to start chopping the tomatoes and slicing the garlic nice and thin. Cook the chicken for 3 minutes or until well coloured, and then flip and cook for a further 3 minutes. Set the chicken aside on a plate. In the same frypan, add the sliced garlic and wine, and cook over high heat for 2 minutes or until the liquid is almost all gone. Then add the chopped tomatoes, chicken stock and oregano. Cook over high heat again for 5 minutes, stirring, and return the chicken to the pan. Reduce the heat to low, partially cover the pan and simmer for about 15 minutes. Season with salt and pepper, and serve with boiled potatoes or rice.

Riso con Pollo

4	chicken thighs	4
1	small onion	1
2	cloves garlic	2
2	tomatoes	2
	A handful of parsley	
	Salt	
	Pepper	
1 tbsp	vegetable oil	15 mL
1 cup	long-grain rice	250 mL
½ cup	white wine	125 mL
1 cup	water	250 mL

While one of you takes care of the chicken, the other can start chopping the onion, garlic, tomatoes and parsley. Sprinkle the chicken thighs with salt and pepper. Heat the oil in a frypan over medium-high heat, and add the chicken, skin side down. Cook for 3 minutes, and then turn them over and cook for 3 more minutes. Remove the chicken from the pan, and set aside. In the same frypan, add the chopped onion and garlic. Cook for 3–4 minutes, until the onion starts to turn clear. While someone stirs, add the rice, and cook for 1 minute (keep stirring!) or until the rice is well coated and starting to turn clear. Add the tomatoes, wine and water, cover and reduce the heat to medium low. Simmer for 10 minutes, and then place the chicken back into the pan and cook for another 10 minutes, covered. Remove the pan from the heat, sprinkle the mixture with parsley and let it sit, covered again, while someone sets the table.

Princess Pamela's Fried Chicken

Princess Pamela
fed me dinner in
New York City in
the 1970s.

	Lots of vegetable oil (not olive)	
1	egg	1
½ cup	milk	125 mL
1 cup	flour	250 mL
½ tsp	salt	2 mL
¼ cup	cornmeal	50 mL
1 tsp	baking powder	5 mL
	A pinch of pepper	
	A pinch of paprika	
6	pieces chicken	6
	(3 legs and 3 thighs are good)	
1	tin (14 oz/398 mL) peaches drained	1
	Juice of 1 lemon	
½ cup	water	125 mL
3 tbsp	brown sugar	45 mL
1 tbsp	butter	15 mL
1 tbsp	white vinegar	15 mL
½ tsp	paprika	2 mL
	A pinch of salt	
	A pinch of cayenne	

Heat the oil 1 inch (2.5 cm) deep in a high-sided saucepan over medium-high heat. As the oil heats, mix the egg and milk together in one bowl, and the flour, salt, cornmeal, baking powder, pepper and paprika in another bowl. Dip the chicken pieces into the milk mixture first, and then into the flour. Fry the chicken pieces in the oil until golden brown, turning them over if necessary. While the chicken cooks, have someone combine the remaining ingredients in a saucepan over medium heat and cook it until it just starts to boil. Drain the chicken pieces on paper towels and let them cool for a minute, then serve immediately with the sauce.

Cooking for Two

Eight-Hour Chicken

1	small roasting chicken	1	
	Salt		
	Pepper		
	Aluminum foil		
1	small onion	1	
	A splash of wine or water		
½ cup	whipping cream	125 mL	

Go to a movie or massage class while dinner cooks — it won't burn.

*P*reheat your oven to 200°F (95°C). Rub the chicken all over with salt and pepper, and wrap it loosely in foil. Place it in a roasting pan in the oven. Let it cook for 8 hours. Remove the chicken from the oven, and tear a hole near the bottom of the tin foil. Pour the pan juices from the chicken into a saucepan, and cook over medium heat. Have someone finely chop the onion while you set the chicken aside, with the foil still over top. Add the onion to the saucepan, and bring the pan juices to a boil. Add a splash of wine (and pour some for yourselves, too), reduce the heat to low and simmer the mixture for about 5 minutes. In the meantime, get someone to start carving the chicken. Stir the cream into the simmering sauce, season with salt and pepper, and serve.

Rye Chicken

3 tbsp	vegetable oil	45 mL
1	small onion	1
2	cloves garlic	2
	A sprig of tarragon	
4–6	chicken thighs	4–6
	(depending on how hungry you are)	
2 oz	rye whisky	60 mL

Heat the oil in a frypan over medium-high heat while someone chops the onion, garlic and tarragon. Add the onion and garlic to the frypan, and cook for 2 minutes or until the onion starts to turn clear. Push the onions and garlic to one side, and lay the chicken pieces in the pan. Cook for 2–3 minutes on each side or until golden brown, and then add the rye and tarragon. Reduce the heat to medium, cover and cook for 15 minutes (check it a couple of times, and if the rye evaporates, just add a bit of water or more rye to the pan). Remove the lid, cook for 1 minute and serve.

CHICKEN WITH CHERRY TOMATOES AND GINGER

2 tbsp	vegetable oil	30 mL
2	skinless boneless chicken breasts	2
1 inch	fresh ginger	2.5 cm
2	cloves garlic	2
1 pint	cherry tomatoes (about 15)	500 mL
¼ cup	water	50 mL
1 cup	frozen peas, still frozen	250 mL
	Salt	
	Pepper	

Heat the oil in a frypan over medium-high heat. While someone cuts the chicken into bite-sized pieces, finely chop the ginger and garlic. Add the chicken, ginger and garlic to the frypan, and cook for 4–5 minutes, until the chicken starts to change colour. Add the whole cherry tomatoes, water and peas. Cover and cook for another 3 minutes or until the peas are done but still crisp. Season with salt and pepper, and eat immediately.

Sort-of Souvlaki

2	skinless boneless chicken breasts	2
	A sprig of oregano	
¼ cup	good olive oil	50 mL
	Juice of 1 lemon	
4	wooden skewers	4
	Salt	
	Pepper	
1	tomato	1
½	long English cucumber	½
½ cup	yogurt	125 mL
	Pita bread	

While you cut the chicken into bite-sized pieces, have someone chop the oregano and mix it with the oil and lemon juice in a shallow dish. Soak the skewers in water for a few minutes, then thread the chicken pieces onto the skewers, and season the chicken with a little salt and pepper. Let the skewers sit in the marinade, refrigerated, for a couple of hours. If you are using a barbecue, let it heat up for 30–40 minutes before putting the skewers on it. Otherwise, heat a frypan over medium-high heat for 5 minutes before putting the skewers in it. Cook the chicken for 6–8 minutes, brushing more of the marinade on it while it cooks, and turning once. While you are doing this, have someone chop the tomato and cucumber, and stir them into the yogurt. Serve the souvlaki with the yogurt mixture on the side, and with some fresh pita bread.

CHICKEN AL CONQUISTADOR

2 tbsp	vegetable oil	25 mL
2	skinless boneless chicken breasts	2
	A slice of good bread, preferably stale	
⅓ cup	light cream	75 mL
1	small onion	1
2	cloves garlic	2
2 tsp	ground cumin	10 mL
	A pinch of cinnamon	
	Salt	
	Pepper	
1	sweet red pepper	1
1–2	small green chili peppers	1–2
2	tomatoes	2
1 cup	chicken stock or water	250 mL
	A few sprigs of cilantro or parsley	
	A handful of large black pitted olives	

This is a Peruvian dish, with a splash of Spanish flavour.

Heat the oil in a frypan over medium-high heat. While you cut the chicken into thin slivers, have someone soak the bread in the cream in a small bowl. Add the chicken to the frypan, and let it cook for 2 minutes. In the meantime, chop the onion and garlic, and add it to the frypan. Stir in the spices and bread mixture, and cook for about 3–4 minutes while someone chops the peppers and tomatoes. Add the peppers, tomatoes and stock to the pan, cover and reduce the heat to low. Let everything simmer for about 20 minutes. While it's cooking, put on some rice, set the table, pour yourself a glass of wine and chop the cilantro. Just before serving, stir in the olives and chopped cilantro. Serve over rice.

CHICKEN NORMANDE

A Saturday evening supper – you spent all morning shopping for Calvados.

2 tbsp	vegetable oil	25 mL
4	chicken thighs	4
2	medium apples	2
2 tbsp	butter	25 mL
¼ tsp	cinnamon	1 mL
	Salt	
	Pepper	
½ cup	light cream	125 mL
2 oz	Calvados (apple brandy)	50 mL
	or whisky or apple juice or cider	

Heat the oil in a frypan over medium-high heat. While you brown the chicken thighs on both sides, have someone peel, core and slice the apples. Remove the chicken from the pan, and add the butter. Reduce the heat to medium, lay the sliced apples in the pan, and cook them gently for 5 minutes. Sprinkle them with cinnamon, and lay the chicken on top of the apples. Season with salt and pepper, pour in the cream and cover the pan. Reduce the heat to medium low, and let everything simmer for 15 minutes. Pour in the Calvados, and cook for a further 5 minutes, covered.

Moroccan Chicken

	A handful of mint	
	A pinch of cinnamon	
	A pinch of cayenne	
1 tsp	lemon zest	5 mL
1 tbsp	fresh lemon juice	15 mL
2	skinless, boneless chicken breasts	2
10	dried apricots	10
2 oz	dried dates	50 g
¼ cup	white wine	50 mL
1	piece (6 oz/150 g) frozen puff pastry, thawed	1
1	egg	1
1 tbsp	milk	15 mL
½ tsp	superfine sugar	2 mL

Preheat your oven to 400°F (200°C). Chop the mint, and combine it with the cinnamon, cayenne, lemon zest and juice. Marinate the chicken in this mixture while preparing the other ingredients (or overnight if you can). Chop the apricots and dates, and cook them with the wine in a small pot over low heat until most of the wine has been absorbed. Have someone roll the pastry out to a ⅛-inch (3 mm) thickness, and cut tops to fit two individual casserole dishes. Meanwhile, you can butter the casserole dishes, place one chicken breast in each and cover with the fruit. Then mix the egg and milk together. Place the pastry over top of the casserole dishes, and brush with the egg wash. Dust the top of the pastry with sugar, and bake, uncovered, for 20 minutes or until the pastry is nicely browned and the chicken is cooked through.

LAMB

I talk a lot about the sensual aspects of food, how it's warm and comforting, smooth and sharp, soft and gentle, ripe and sunny. And all the words I use (or anybody else uses) about food are positive. They're all supportive and nourishing words, long-lasting and familiar words, really loving words.

People laugh at the Jewish mother syndrome ("Eat, eat."). But this need to feed people is not just Jewish. We all do it — we all want to nourish somebody else and nourish ourselves. That's why we give parties — it's not just to get a few drinks down or look around to see if there's somebody interesting we just might get to know. It's a way of giving comfort or, even more, giving a few hugs that we otherwise might be embarrassed about. You can't walk up and throw your arms round a complete stranger at a party, but you can suggest he or she tries the liver pâté or the crab, and then you can look a little proud and say that you made it, and would they like some more, and all of a sudden, there you are, talking like old friends.

This approach seems to work with only home-made food. Opening a packet just isn't the same. There's no love in it, no romance, no intimacy and no sense of adventure.

Cooking does something special. There's a word for it in classical French cooking: *le mariage* (the marriage). It means the slow coming together of separate things. The process takes time and a little work. We've all heard that before. "Marriage isn't easy," say our friends, our mothers and our counsellors. "You gotta work at it. You can't just get it off the shelf — you gotta be patient."

It doesn't have to be complicated. You don't have to rush out and take gourmet cooking lessons to make your love life work. But if you cook something, anything, from scratch, rather than ripping open a packet, adding water and stirring, you just might find that things start to get better — kids, spouses, in-laws, even the cat will look at you with respect, gratitude or at least curiosity. Much cheaper than counselling.

Lamb is a good thing to start being adventurous with — in a stew or on a barbecue or even in a lamburger. It *marries* well with almost anything: tomatoes, most herbs, apples, potatoes, garlic, red wine, peppers, and beans. I once ate a wonderful stew of lamb and peanuts in Northern China, and since then I've taken to spreading peanut butter on barbecued lamb chops.

Lamb Shanks

2	lamb shanks	2
	Salt	
	Pepper	
¼ cup	olive oil	50 mL
1	lemon	1
1 tsp	turmeric	5 mL
½ cup	water	125 mL

Sprinkle the lamb shanks with salt and pepper. Heat 1 tbsp (15 mL) of the oil in a pot over medium-high heat. Add the lamb shanks, and cook them until they're browned all over, about 2 minutes on each side. In the meantime, have someone juice the lemon and mix together the juice with the turmeric and water. When the shanks are browned, drizzle the remaining olive oil over top of them, along with the lemon juice mixture. Cover the pot, reduce the heat to medium and bring to a boil. Reduce the heat again to the lowest setting, and simmer, covered, for about 1½ hours. Check the pot now and then, and add a bit of water if the liquid has evaporated.

CHELO

2 tbsp	vegetable oil	25 mL	
1 lb	stewing lamb	450 g	
8–10	dried apricots	8–10	
1	clove garlic	1	
1	large carrot	1	
½ tsp	cinnamon	2 mL	
1 cup	water	250 mL	
½ tsp	salt	2 mL	
⅛ tsp	pepper	1 mL	
	A handful of whole blanched almonds		

A Turkish dish that I discovered in Paris. One of those "better the next day" dishes.

While you heat the oil in a stockpot over medium-high heat, have someone chop the lamb into bite-sized pieces. Add the lamb to the pot, and brown it quickly on all sides. Chop the apricots, garlic and carrot, and add them to the pot. Stir in the cinnamon, water, salt and pepper, and reduce the heat to low. Let the whole thing simmer, covered, for 2 hours while you go on a bird-watching jaunt or to your weekly bridge game. Just before serving, toast the almonds in a dry frypan over medium heat. Let the almonds cool a bit (so you don't burn your hands when you chop them), and serve the stew with the chopped almonds sprinkled over top.

A Nice Lamb Stew for the Middle of Winter

1	tin (19 oz/540 mL) brown lentils	1
1	small onion	1
2	cloves garlic	2
	A couple of fresh sage leaves	
3	tomatoes	3
8 oz	stewing lamb	250 g
2 tbsp	vegetable oil	25 mL
	Salt	
	Pepper	
2 cups	water	500 mL

*D*rain and rinse the lentils under cold running water. Preheat your oven to 350°F (180°F), and have someone chop the onion, garlic, sage and tomatoes while you cut the lamb into bite-sized pieces. Heat the oil in an ovenproof pot over medium-high heat. Add the lamb, and cook it for 3 minutes, until it is browned on all sides. Add the lentils, onion, garlic, sage, tomatoes, salt, pepper and water to the pot, stir it all together, cover it and put it in the oven. Let it cook for 1½ hours or until the lamb is tender and the lentils have absorbed most of the water (check the pot every half hour to make sure the stew doesn't get too dry — if it does, just add another cup of water).

LAMB BURGERS

	A couple of sprigs of parsley	
½	medium onion	½
	A couple of sprigs of rosemary	
2	cloves garlic	2
10 oz	ground lamb	300 g
2 tbsp	bread crumbs	25 mL
1	egg	1
2 tsp	Dijon mustard	10 mL
¼ tsp	salt	1 mL
	A pinch of pepper	

Please don't run around heaven's half acre looking for ground lamb. Call your local butcher ahead of time and ask him or her to prepare some for you. While one of you has gone to pick up the lamb, the other can finely chop the parsley, onion, rosemary and garlic. Pre-heat your oven to 400°F (200°C). Combine all of the ingredients, and form into two patties. You can fry them if you like, but roasting them in the oven is easier, and it gives you a better opportunity to get rid of some excess fat. Place the patties in an ungreased baking pan, and roast for 25 minutes. Then pour off the fat, return the pan to the oven and broil for 5 minutes. You can serve them with all the traditional hamburger fixings or try a little tzatziki with them.

PORK AND BEEF

Cooking is a lot easier than it's made out to be. A lot of people don't cook because they've been scared off — they failed Peanut Butter Cookies in Grade 8 because they didn't measure in level spoonfuls and they never wanted to go near a kitchen again. The one thing home economics teachers never manage to tell their students is to relax. Having a tidy kitchen is not the main purpose of making dinner — you don't have to be continually polishing the saucepans. Carpenters don't do that with their hammers. They bang in a few nails and put it the hammer back in their apron until it's time to bang in some more, and if the nice new hammer collects a few nicks and scratches along the way, then that's just fine — it looks like a real hammer, not a piece of art.

Cooking is a craft as much as an art, but it's also a very natural thing to do. Food is food. It's nourishment *and* pleasure, and all recipes are originally the fruit of somebody's imagination. Imagination doesn't work if you're worried. So there it is: if you want to cook, just stop worrying. The next step is to see what you've got, instead of what you ought to have. That's the way artists work. They do what they can with what they've got, and they try not to let things get too complicated.

Basically there are only four recipes in the world. You take your food home — whether you've hunted it or bought it or grown it doesn't matter — and then, whether you're British or French or

Chinese or Italian, there are basically four things you can do with it. You can bake it, boil it, fry it or screw it up. All cooking is a variation on one of these procedures. The most important of North American philosophers was Henry Thoreau, and he said, "Beware any venture requiring new clothes." You, in the kitchen, should beware any recipe requiring new and super-sophisticated equipment.

The next thing to remember is that God, when she made the world, developed a very simple kitchen principle: The things that grow together go together. That's why Italian food is the way it is — tomatoes, garlic and veal grow in Italy, with oregano wild on the hillsides. Chinese food is largely based on pork and duck because pigs and ducks are the most efficient animals there are for converting what they eat into meat that we can eat. Beans and corn in Mexico, fish in Japan — that's what they've got, so that's what they cook with. In Brittany they've got lots  of cows and apple orchards and pigs that eat the apples, so their cooking uses lots of cream and Calvados and pork.

Cooking doesn't come out of a book — it develops. Food originally was a necessity as basic as gas for a car, and then people got knives and forks to use instead of their teeth and fingers, and suddenly there was pepper and salt and maître d's and flowers on the table — all kinds of ideas about how to make things nice and pleasing. But the important thing was to learn how to make changes. If you had always cooked dinosaurs and then suddenly they weren't around any more, then you had to start using pterodactyls right?

Pork and Beef

So if you want to develop a recipe, you take what you've got. Meat is meat. If the recipe calls for veal and you haven't got it or can't afford it, then use pork. Or chicken. Take a recipe like piccata de vitello, a very famous Italian dish. It calls for a slice of veal cut very thin, fried quickly in butter and then doused with lemon juice and a little white wine, some pepper and salt. I use chicken breasts instead of veal, beaten thin between lightly floured wax paper, and sometimes I use pork, also beaten thin. Nobody knows the difference because people who come to dinner are not gourmets. They're just grateful. They get a free supper, and they haven't got to do the dishes. If the recipe calls for cider and you haven't got cider, then use apple juice. Or even beer. It will taste a bit different, but it will still taste nice.

So think of a few basic rules, and you'll be able to invent your own recipes. Think of things like contrast. We all like sweet and sour soup, and the same principle applies to other food. Almost any soup you've made that tastes flat will pick up enormously with a teaspoonful of vinegar (or lemon juice) added, for the last two minutes of cooking. A pinch of sugar — not a great heaping spoonful, just a pinch — does wonders for vegetables like Brussels sprouts. If you make a vinaigrette, the basic salad dressings, to brighten up a bit of old lettuce, stir a little curry powder or half a teaspoon of thyme into it. Just learn to ignore what your mother told you, and play with your food. You'll enjoy it more.

Cuban Pork Stew

8 oz	pork tenderloin	250 g
1	small onion	1
1	sweet green pepper	1
2	cloves garlic	2
1	tomato	1
3 tbsp	flour	45 mL
2 tbsp	vegetable oil	25 mL
1	small green chili pepper	1
½ tsp	ground cumin	2 mL
½ glass	white wine or apple juice	125 mL
1 cup	chicken stock	250 mL
1	banana	1
	A handful of cilantro	
	Salt	
	Pepper	

One person cooks while the other chops. While you cut the pork into 1-inch (2.5 cm) chunks, have someone chop the onion, green pepper, garlic and tomato. Place the flour in a shallow dish, and roll the pork in it until all of the pieces are well coated. Heat the oil in a large pot over high heat. Add the pork, and cook until browned on all sides, about 3–4 minutes. Add the chopped onion, whole chili pepper and chopped green pepper to the pot, and cook for about 3 minutes, stirring, until the onion starts to turn clear. Add the garlic, and cook for another 2 minutes. Add the cumin, wine, chopped tomato and stock. Stir everything together, and let it come to a boil. Reduce the heat to low, and let the stew simmer, covered, for 15 minutes. In the meantime, put some rice on to cook, and set the table. Chop the banana and cilantro, add them to the stew and cook it for another 5 minutes. Season with salt and pepper, and serve with the cooked rice.

ARGENTINE FLANK STEAK

Flank steak is best when marinated for half an hour before cooking. Makes it melt in your mouth.

1	clove garlic	1
¼ cup	red wine	50 mL
1 tbsp	vegetable oil	15 mL
1 lb	flank steak or skirt steak	450 g

CHIMICHURRI SAUCE — A SPICY SALSA

1	small onion	1
1	sweet green pepper	1
1	tomato	1
1	clove garlic	1
1	small green chili pepper	1
	A handful of parsley	
2 tbsp	white vinegar	25 mL
2 tbsp	vegetable oil	25 mL
	A handful of cilantro	
	Salt	
	Pepper	

*C*hop the garlic while someone mixes the red wine and oil in a shallow dish. Stir in the garlic and lay the flank steak in the dish. Let it sit for half an hour, turning occasionally, while you make the sauce.

Cut the onion, green pepper, tomato and garlic coarsely, so they will fit into a food processor (if you do not have a food processor, chop everything, including the herbs, fine). Combine all of the sauce ingredients except the salt and pepper in the food processor, and blend until finely chopped. Season with salt and pepper, and set aside. After the steak has marinated, heat a small amount of oil in a frypan over high heat. Get someone to set the table and pour the wine. Remove the flank steak from the marinade, and add it to the hot frypan. Cook it for about 3 minutes on each side for a medium-rare steak. Remove the steak from the pan, and slice it into thin strips diagonally across its width (against the grain). Serve the slices with the sauce on the side. Great with boiled new potatoes.

PLAIN AND SIMPLE
ROASTED PORK CHOPS

2 tbsp	vegetable oil	25 mL
2	thick pork chops	2
2	medium apples	2
1	lemon	1
3	cloves garlic	3
	Salt	
	Pepper	

Preheat your oven to 450°F (230°C). Heat the oil in an ungreased ovenproof frypan over medium-high heat. Add the pork chops, and cook for 2 minutes on each side, just until browned. While you are browning the pork chops, have someone quarter the apples and core them. Place the apples in the frypan. Cut the lemon in half, squeeze the juice over top and place the lemon halves in the frypan too. Smash the garlic cloves with the back of a knife, and add them to the pan. Season with salt and pepper. Bake, covered, for 20–25 minutes, while you watch the news or cut the grass or call your aunt. Remove the pork chops from the oven, let them rest for about 5 minutes and then eat!

SAUSAGE AND BEANS

2 tbsp	vegetable oil	25 mL
1	small onion	1
2	cloves garlic	2
1	small green chili pepper	1
2	tomatoes	2
2	spicy or mild Italian sausages	2
1	tin (28 oz/796 mL) white (cannellini or navy) beans	1
½ cup	water	125 mL
	A handful of parsley	
	Salt	
	Pepper	

Heat the oil in a large frypan over medium-high heat. While you chop the onion, garlic, chili pepper and tomato, have someone slice the sausages into coins ½-inch (1 cm) thick. Add the sliced sausage, and cook for 5–6 minutes. Add the chopped onion, garlic, chili pepper and tomato to the frypan, and cook for 3–4 minutes, stirring, until the onion starts to turn clear and the tomato begins to fall apart. In the meantime, have someone open the can of beans and rinse and drain them. When the sausage is no longer pink, add the beans and water and give it all a big stir. Reduce the heat to medium, cover and let the whole lot cook for another 3–4 minutes. Chop the parsley, sprinkle it over top, season with salt and pepper, and serve.

BEEF BROCHETTES

2–4	wooden skewers	2–4
8 oz	beef tenderloin	250 g
	A sprig of rosemary	
1	small onion	1
2	tomatoes	2
2 tbsp	vegetable oil	25 mL
2 tbsp	Dijon mustard	25 mL
	Salt	
	Pepper	
¼ cup	water	50 mL

Soak the skewers in water for a few minutes. While you cut the beef into bite-sized pieces and thread them onto the skewers, have some-one chop the rosemary, onion and tomatoes. Heat the oil in a frypan over medium-high heat. Brush a thin layer of mustard on the beef, and place the skewers in the frypan to brown each side. Add the chopped onion and tomato, and cook for 2–3 minutes. Stir the veg-etables, and turn the skewers over. Sprinkle with rosemary and a little salt and pepper, and cook the beef for another 2 minutes. Remove the beef from the pan, and set aside. Add the water to the pan, and bring the tomato mixture to a boil. Pour the sauce over the beef, and serve. Great with mashed potatoes.

Two-Meat Meatballs

8 oz	ground beef	250 g
8 oz	ground lamb	250 g
1	small onion	1
	A handful of cilantro	
	A thick slice of white bread	
	A pinch of cinnamon	
	Salt	
	Pepper	
½ tsp	cumin seeds or ground cumin	2 mL
1 cup	plain yogurt	250 mL
1 tbsp	vegetable oil	15 mL

Combine all of the ingredients except the cumin, yogurt and oil in a food processor, and mix until well combined. While you commission someone to roll the meat into ping pong–sized balls, warm a dry frypan over medium heat. Add the cumin seeds to the pan, toasting them until you can smell their spiciness. Stir the cumin into the yogurt, and set the yogurt aside. Reduce the heat to medium. In the same frypan, heat the oil, add the meatballs and cook them until browned on all sides, about 8 minutes. Serve with the yogurt as a dipping sauce.

Korma

8 oz	pork or beef tenderloin	250 g	A mild, gentle and rich curry.
2	cloves garlic	2	
½ cup	plain yogurt	125 mL	
½ tsp	turmeric	2 mL	
2 tbsp	vegetable oil	25 mL	
1	small onion	1	
2	whole cloves	2	
½ tsp	pepper	2 mL	
½ tsp	cinnamon	2 mL	
	A pinch of salt		
¼ cup	water	50 mL	

Get someone to cut the pork into bite-sized pieces while you chop the garlic. Mix the meat, garlic, yogurt and turmeric together in a bowl, and let it sit, refrigerated, for anywhere between 2 and 6 hours. After you have done that, heat the oil in a frypan over medium-high heat while someone chops the onion. Add the onion, spices and salt to the pan, and cook for 2–3 minutes. Then add the meat and yogurt mixture and the water, stir it all together, cover the pan and let it cook for 45 minutes. Check on it once in awhile, making sure it doesn't get too dry (if it does, just add more water). Discard the cloves. Serve with rice or chapatis or chickpeas.

Pork Chops for the Upper Crust

Chicken breasts cook in half the time if your in-laws don't eat pork.

¼ tsp	pepper	2 mL
2 tsp	Dijon mustard	10 mL
1 tsp	salt	5 mL
1 tbsp	vegetable oil	15 mL
1 tbsp	butter	15 mL
4	small pork chops (or 2 thick ones)	4
1	small onion	1
1 cup	white wine	250 mL
	A couple of sprigs of parsley	

Mix together the pepper, mustard and salt while someone heats the oil and butter in a frypan over medium heat. Spread the mustard mixture on both sides of the pork chops. Chop the onion fine, and add it to the frypan. Cook for 2 minutes, then shove it to one side of the pan and add the pork chops. Brown the pork chops on both sides, cooking them for about 2 minutes on each side. Add the wine, and reduce the heat to low. Cover the frypan, and let the pork chops cook for 45 minutes. When you are ready to eat, chop the parsley, sprinkle it over the pork chops and serve. Terrific over egg noodles or leftover pasta.

PORTUGUESE PORK AND CLAMS

3 tbsp	vegetable oil	45 mL	**Almost as good with canned clams.**
1 lb	pork tenderloin	450 g	
1	small onion	1	
1	stalk celery	1	
2	cloves garlic	2	
1	sweet green pepper	1	
2	tomatoes	2	
½ cup	white wine	125 mL	
1	bay leaf	1	
	A pinch of paprika		
12	small fresh clams, in the shell	12	
	A couple of sprigs of cilantro		

While you heat the oil in a saucepan over medium-high heat and cut the pork into bite-sized pieces, have someone chop the onion, celery, garlic, green pepper and tomatoes. Add the pork to the saucepan, and cook until browned on all sides, about 6 minutes. Remove the pork from the saucepan, and set aside. In the same saucepan, cook the chopped vegetables for 2–3 minutes, then add the wine, bay leaf and paprika, and cook for a further 10 minutes. Add the clams, cover the saucepan and cook until the clams have opened, about 8 minutes or so. Discard any clams that did not open. In the meantime, chop the cilantro. Return the pork to the saucepan, and cook for another 2 minutes. Discard the bay leaf and serve with the chopped cilantro sprinkled over top.

MABO DON

A real comfort
food, Asian style.

2 tbsp	vegetable oil	25 mL
1 inch	fresh ginger	2.5 cm
2	cloves garlic	2
1 tbsp	red pepper flakes	15 mL
4 oz	lean ground pork or beef	100 g
2	green onions	2
½ lb	medium or firm tofu	250 g
2 tbsp	soy sauce	25 mL
½ cup	water	125 mL
1 tsp	flour or cornstarch	5 mL
	Sesame oil	

Heat the oil in a wok or high-sided frypan over high heat. Have someone finely chop the ginger and garlic. Add them with the red pepper
flakes to the wok, and cook, stirring constantly, for 1 minute. Then
add the pork, and cook for 2–3 minutes, stirring to break up the
clumps of meat. In the meantime, have someone chop the green
onions and cut the tofu into small cubes. Add the green onions and
tofu to the wok, and cook for 2 minutes, stirring. Mix together the
soy sauce, water and flour in a small bowl, and pour into the wok. The
mixture will thicken as soon as it boils (almost right away). Stir and
serve with a bit of sesame oil drizzled over top.

CABBAGE AND SAUSAGES

1 tbsp	vegetable oil	15 mL
2	mild or spicy Italian sausages	2
1	small onion	1
1	clove garlic	1
1	small head cabbage	1
½ cup	water	125 mL
	Salt	
	Pepper	

While you heat the oil in a high-sided frypan, have someone slice the sausages into ½-inch (1 cm) thick coins, and chop the onion, garlic and cabbage. Lay the sliced sausage in the pan, and cook for 1 minute on each side. Push the sausage to one side of the pan, and add the onion and garlic, cooking for 2 minutes, until the onion begins to turn clear. Add the cabbage, and stir the whole lot, so that most of the sausage winds up on top of the cabbage. Reduce the heat to medium, add the water and season with salt and pepper. Cover the pan, and cook until the cabbage has wilted, about 8–10 minutes.

Beef and Oranges

8 oz	flank steak or skirt steak	250 g
1 tsp	cornstarch	5 mL
1 tbsp	soy sauce	15 mL
	Pepper	
2 tbsp	vegetable oil	25 mL
1 inch	fresh ginger	2.5 cm
2	cloves garlic	2
1	orange	1
1 tsp	dried chili peppers	5 mL
1 cup	cherry tomatoes	250 mL

Slice the steak thinly, against the grain, and place in a bowl. Mix the cornstarch, soy sauce, pepper and 1 tbsp (15 mL) of the oil, and pour the mixture over the beef. Heat the other tablespoon of oil in a frypan over medium-high heat. While you grate the ginger and chop the garlic, have someone zest the orange or cut thin strips of the peel off and chop them up. Add the ginger and garlic to the frypan, and stir. Add the beef (and its marinade), orange zest, chili peppers and tomatoes. Cut the orange in half and squeeze the juice into the pan. Stir and cook for 6 minutes or so, or until the beef is cooked and a nice sauce has formed in the pan.

Pork Loin in Phyllo Pastry

2 tbsp	ginger marmalade	25 mL
10 oz	pork tenderloin	300 g
3	sheets frozen phyllo pastry	3
2 tbsp	butter, melted	25 mL
	Salt	
	Pepper	

Rub the marmalade into the pork, and let it sit overnight in the refrigerator. Take the phyllo pastry out of the freezer to thaw about half an hour before starting. Preheat your oven to 375°F (190°C). While one of you greases a baking sheet and cuts the pork into two servings, the other can prepare the pastry. Lay one sheet of phyllo on the counter, and brush it with melted butter. Lay a second sheet over the first, and brush it with butter. Lay the third sheet over the second, and (can you guess?) brush it with butter. Cut the pastry widthwise into two equal pieces, and place a piece of pork in the centre of each pastry square. Season the pork with salt and pepper, wrap it in the pastry and brush butter onto the folds. Place each bundle onto the baking sheet, seam side down, brush the top with butter and bake for 30 minutes or until the pastry is golden and the pork is cooked through.

tomorrow (dump in a glass of wine and a little chopped parsley to freshen it up). Garlic is okay at supper, so is the occasional burp and people who come to supper are generally nicer. So . . . one dish and a nice salad.

Moroccan Orange and Radish Salad

1	bunch radishes	1	
2	oranges	2	
	Salt		
	Pepper		
3 tbsp	olive oil	45 mL	

Slice the radishes thinly, and arrange them on a serving plate while someone peels and chops the oranges. Scatter the oranges over the radishes. Sprinkle with salt and pepper, and drizzle the olive oil over top. Serve.

Romaine Hearts with Olive Oil

1	head romaine lettuce	1	
¼ cup	olive oil	50 mL	
	Salt		
	Pepper		

Tear away the leaves on the head of lettuce until you reach the "heart" (about halfway through, where the leaves start getting much lighter in colour). Reserve the outer leaves for another use, and cut the heart into wedges lengthwise. Divide the wedges between two serving plates. Sprinkle the wedges with olive oil, salt and pepper, and serve.

Grand Aioli

A home-made garlic mayonnaise dip for fresh vegetables.	2	cloves garlic	2
	1	egg yolk	1
	1 cup	olive oil	250 mL
		Juice of 1 lemon	

Chop the garlic as fine as you can. In a food processor, beat the egg yolk and garlic together until the egg has thickened and is pale yellow. With the processor still running, continue to beat the egg yolk, and have someone pour the oil into the mixture in a very slow, thin stream. The mixture should stay thick and turn white (slow down the pouring of the oil if it is not all being absorbed as it is being poured). Beat in the lemon juice, and serve as a salad dressing or with cherry tomatoes, steamed new potatoes or broccoli, or any of your favourite vegetables.

Green Bean Salad

1 lb	green beans	450 g
½ cup	vegetable oil	125 mL
¼ cup	white vinegar	50 mL
1 tsp	Dijon mustard	5 mL
½ tsp	tarragon	2 mL
	Salt	
	Pepper	
	A pinch of white sugar	

Bring a large pot of water to a boil. In the meantime, trim the ends of the green beans, and place the beans in the boiling water. Let them cook for about 6 minutes, while someone makes the dressing: combine the remaining ingredients together in a large jar, and shake it until the dressing is smooth. Set it aside. Drain the beans, and rinse them under cold running water. Toss with the dressing, and serve.

Fatima's Carrot Salad

Fatima was a beautiful, bright-eyed vegetarian.

2	large carrots	2
1	clove garlic	1
	A couple of sprigs of parsley	
½ tsp	ground cumin or cumin seeds	2 mL
¼ tsp	paprika	1 mL
	A pinch of cinnamon	
	A pinch of cayenne	
	Salt	
	A squeeze of lemon juice	
¼ cup	olive oil	50 mL

*B*ring a pot of water to a boil over high heat. While you peel and chop the carrots into bite-sized wedges, have someone chop the garlic and parsley. Cook the carrots until tender, about 5 minutes, and then rinse them under cold water. Combine the rest of the ingredients, as well as the chopped garlic and parsley, to make a marinade. Drain the carrots, and add them to the marinade. Let the salad sit for about an hour, and then serve.

GREENS WITH WARM PEAR AND WALNUT DRESSING

	2 handfuls baby greens or any mixed greens	
1 ½ oz	blue cheese	37 g
1	pear	1
2 tbsp	crushed walnuts	25 mL
1 tsp	butter	5 mL
2 tbsp	port or wine vinegar	25 mL
3 tbsp	olive oil	45 mL
	Salt	
	Pepper	

Wash the greens, spin or pat them dry, and portion them into two salad bowls. Crumble the blue cheese on top. Meanwhile have someone peel, core and cube the pear, and then sauté the pear cubes with the walnuts in butter over medium heat until the pear cubes are lightly browned. Add the wine to the pan, and when it begins to bubble, remove the saucepan from the heat, and whisk in the olive oil. Season with salt and pepper. Serve the dressing while it is still warm, over the greens and cheese.

HOLIDAY DINNERS FOR TWO

*O*ctober is Thanksgiving time in the Northern Hemisphere. Everybody is cranking up for some kind of party: a big meal, lots of friends and a lot of sitting round the table and tolerating all the nice lies that come after big family dinners. Sometimes we forget that it really is *Thanksgiving* — the giving of thanks for the harvest. Just about every society does it, one way or another, but it sometimes seems that the more sophisticated we get, the less we appreciate the simple reasons for celebrations.

So we miss out on spontaneous festivals because we insist on having special reasons and arbitrary dates, which we let the national advertisers turn into shopping sprees. The Festival of St. VISA.

In Italy things are very different. There is hardly a village that doesn't have a festival once a month, an excuse for everybody to get out into the streets and whoop it up a bit. They call them *feste* or *sagre*. Everything closes except the bars and restaurants, and even the buses stop running. But on top of all these religion-oriented festivals, there are hundreds of others simply celebrating food. Melons, polenta, asparagus, even beans and onions — they're all celebrated. In Agrigento there is a week-long festival in honour of the flowering almond trees. In Ivrea there's a cabbage soup festival, and the following month (it's still only March) there's a *fagiolate* — one and a half tons of beans and half a ton of sausage.

All the townspeople get involved and cook all night, so they can give it away next day. Most of these fairs are based on simple, honest, innocent food, usually some local specialty (if artichokes grow well in the village, then they have an artichoke celebration, and if their particular piece of the coast has a lot of cod, then it's a cod feast), and everybody eats and eats and eats. Polenta, gnocchi, lasagna. I've even been to a celebration of donkey sausage in Northern Italy. "When the donkey's too old to work, what else you gonna do with 'im?" said my host. In Portugal I've eaten sardine fritters washed down with litres of harsh, blood-red, tooth-staining wine, and in Borgosesia I've eaten tripe for breakfast, lunch and dinner at a tripe festival (the first Tuesday during Lent). They eat so much tripe and drink so much wine on this Tuesday that the town has decided that Wednesday too has to be another festival, a holiday they call *Mercu Scuro*, or Wednesday Obscured, which seems to be a nice way to describe the morning after.

Valentine's Day, the fest of couples, is a prime example of a nice little festival gone wrong. In the week running up to February 14th, more red roses and chocolates are sold than in the rest of the year. The glossy magazines are filled with full colour ads for gooey drinks in fancy bottles, and most hotels offer special Valentine's Day menus, usually consisting of creamy, buttery and indigestible stuff, with the added inducement of a specially priced room for the consummation of the passion supposedly engendered by all this rich food.

I am not entirely without experience in this matter of

consummation, and I know full well that after a bucketful of hollandaise sauce and a couple of Black Russians most people are indeed ready for bed. But almost certainly not for seduction. They want to get horizontal for the strictly utilitarian purpose of sleeping, unless, as is often the case, they are kept from their slumber by indigestion.

The complimentary champagne in the bucket on the dresser, the foil-covered chocolate box, the violets by the bed and the silken minimals that you purchased for this memorable coupling — they mean nothing to an overfilled belly. Far better you should enjoy something light and refreshing, simple and digestible, and then plight your troth without the need for all-night Alka-Seltzer.

If the two of you are making this kind of feast yourselves, you won't want to face a mountain of dishes, so I've devoted this chapter to a collection of easy and simple elegances, which will leave you time and energy to celebrate simply.

Valentine's Day

Thai Papaya Salad

1	clove garlic	1		**Wash and dry**
2	small red chili peppers	2		**papaya seeds**
1	papaya	1		**and use them**
6	cherry tomatoes	6		**as pepper.**
	A handful of bean sprouts			
	A handful of roasted peanuts			
	Juice of 1 lime			
1 tbsp	brown sugar	15 mL		
½ tsp	salt	2 mL		

While someone finely chops the garlic and chili peppers, you can prepare the papaya: cut the papaya in half, scoop out the seeds and cut off the skin. Cube the flesh, and place it in a mixing bowl with the minced garlic and chili peppers. Halve the cherry tomatoes, and add them to the bowl along with the bean sprouts and peanuts. In a small bowl, mix together the lime juice, sugar and salt, and stir until the sugar is dissolved. Pour over the salad, toss and serve.

Laksa

A coconut fish
soup from
Malaysia.

12	unshelled raw prawns	12
2	small red chili peppers	2
2	cloves garlic	2
1 inch	fresh ginger	2.5 cm
	A handful of cilantro	
8 oz	dried Chinese noodles	250 g
2 tbsp	vegetable oil	25 mL
½ tsp	turmeric	2 mL
1	tin (14 oz/398 mL) coconut milk	1
2 cups	water	500 mL
1 tsp	salt	5 mL
	A handful of bean sprouts	

*P*ut a large pot of water on to boil. In the meantime, rinse, peel and devein the prawns, and have someone chop the chili peppers, garlic, ginger and cilantro. Cook the noodles in the boiling water until they are tender, drain them and let them sit in cool water while you prepare the laksa. Heat the oil in a wok over high heat. Add the chili peppers, garlic and ginger, and cook for 1 minute, stirring constantly. Add the prawns, and reduce the heat to medium. Immediately add the turmeric, coconut milk, water and salt. Bring the mixture to a boil. Drain the noodles, and divide them between two serving bowls. Pour the laksa over top, and serve sprinkled with lots of bean sprouts and cilantro.

Five-Spiced Nuts

2 cups	raw almonds, skins on	500 mL
3 tbsp	vegetable oil	45 mL
1 tsp	white sugar	5 mL
1 tsp	Chinese five-spice powder	5 mL

Preheat your oven to 325°F (165°C) and place the almonds in an ungreased baking dish while someone assembles the remaining ingredients. Sprinkle the mixture over top. Stir the almonds about so that they get evenly coated, and then bake them for 10–15 minutes, until nicely browned on the inside. Let cool and serve.

EASTER

HAM FOR TWO

2	tomatoes	2
½ inch	fresh ginger	1 cm
½ cup	apple juice	125 mL
2 tbsp	white vinegar	25 mL
1 tbsp	brown sugar	15 mL
	A pinch of ground cloves	
	Zest of 1 orange	
1	cooked ham steak	1
	(about 12 oz/336 g)	

*P*reheat your oven to 350°F (180°C). Chop the tomatoes and ginger while someone combines the apple juice, vinegar, sugar, cloves and zest. Add the chopped tomatoes and ginger to the mixture. Lay the ham steak in a greased baking dish, and pour the tomato mixture over top. Bake, uncovered, for 25 minutes, spooning a little liquid from the baking dish over the ham now and again. Serve.

Garlic Mashed Potatoes

3	medium potatoes	3
2	cloves garlic	2
¼ cup	light cream	50 mL
2 tbsp	butter	25 mL
1 tsp	salt	5 mL
½ tsp	pepper	2 mL

Put a pot of water on to boil. Peel the potatoes and the garlic and cook them together in boiling water until tender. Drain the potatoes and garlic and place them in a mixing bowl. Mash them a bit with a fork or a potato masher. Stir in the remaining ingredients, and mash until smooth. Serve immediately.

Frozen Grapes

A handful of green seedless grapes
A handful of red seedless grapes
A splash of brandy or sweet wine

Place the grapes on a baking sheet lined with wax paper or paper towels. Put the baking sheet into the freezer, and leave it in there until the grapes are hard (overnight is best). Serve with a little brandy or sweet wine sprinkled over top.

MOTHER'S DAY

WAFFLES

2	eggs, separated	2
2 cups	flour	500 mL
1 tsp	baking powder	5 mL
	A pinch of salt	
2 cups	milk	500 mL
1 tbsp	vegetable oil	15 mL
	Maple syrup	
	Butter	
	Icing sugar	
	Juice of ½ lemon	

Plug in your waffle iron, and let it heat up while you prepare the batter and someone beats the egg whites until stiff. In a large mixing bowl, mix together the flour, baking powder and salt. Stir in the milk, oil and egg yolks, and beat until smooth. Carefully fold in the beaten egg whites. Pour a ladleful of the batter into the greased, preheated waffle iron, and cook for 3–4 minutes, depending on the iron. Serve immediately with maple syrup and butter, or with some icing sugar and lemon juice sprinkled over top. Repeat with the remaining batter.

Banana Smoothies

1	banana	1
1 ½ cups	orange or apple juice	375 mL
½ cup	plain or fruit-flavoured yogurt	125 mL

Combine all of the ingredients in a blender, and mix until smooth. Add more juice for a thinner smoothie, more banana for a thicker one.

Strawberries with Honey and Orange Zest

1 pint	strawberries	500 mL
1 tbsp	honey	15 mL
	Zest of 1 orange	

Remove the stems from the strawberries, and cut the strawberries into halves or quarters. Drizzle with honey, sprinkle with orange zest and serve.

Father's Day

Cucumber Orange Salad

1	long English cucumber	1
	A couple of sprigs of mint	
	A sprig of parsley	
	Zest of ½ orange	
3 tbsp	rice vinegar	45 mL
2 tbsp	white sugar	30 mL

Dice the cucumber and finely chop the mint and parsley. Toss them together in a bowl with the remaining ingredients, and let the salad sit for about half an hour before serving. You can also make this the day before and keep it refrigerated until serving.

LAMB SKEWERS WITH MINT AND YOGURT

etter than
urgers.

1 tbsp	tomato paste	15 mL
½ cup	vegetable oil	125 mL
2 tbsp	brown sugar	25 mL
8 oz	cubed lamb shoulder	250 g
2–4	wooden skewers	2–4
	A sprig of mint	
½ cup	plain yogurt	125 mL

Light your barbecue, and while you wait for it to heat up, stir the
tomato paste, oil and sugar together in a bowl. Add the cubed lamb,
and let it sit in the oil mixture for half an hour. Soak the skewers in
water for a few minutes. When your barbecue is good and hot, thread
the lamb onto skewers, and cook for 3–4 minutes. Turn them over,
and cook for a further 3 minutes. Meanwhile have someone chop the
mint and stir it into the yogurt. Serve the yogurt dip alongside the
lamb skewers.

Apple Crumble

Good next
morning for
breakfast.

	2	medium apples	2
		Zest of 1 lemon	
	¼ cup	white sugar	50 mL
	2 tbsp	flour	25 mL
	3 tbsp	cold butter	45 mL
	⅓ cup	flour	75 mL
	⅓ cup	brown sugar	75 mL
		A pinch of salt	
	¼ tsp	cinnamon	1 mL

*P*reheat your oven (or barbecue) to 350°F (180°C). While you peel, core and chop the apples, have someone grease a baking tin. Toss the apples, lemon zest, white sugar and 2 tbsp (25 mL) flour together, and put the mixture in the tin. In a bowl, rub the butter and ⅓ cup (75 mL) flour together with your hands until you have a crumbly mixture (with no lumps of butter). Stir in the brown sugar, salt and cinnamon, and spread the topping over the apples. Bake for 25–30 minutes, until the apples have softened. (If you are cooking it on your barbecue, cover the baking tin with some foil and bake for 25–30 minutes well above the flame.)

THANKSGIVING

MIXED GREENS WITH VINAIGRETTE

2 cups	mixed greens or lettuce	500 mL
¼ cup	good olive oil	50 mL
1 tsp	dry mustard	5 mL
2 tbsp	white vinegar	25 mL
	A pinch of white sugar	
	A pinch of salt	
½ tsp	pepper	2 mL

Tear the lettuce into bite-sized pieces, if necessary. While you do this, have someone mix the oil and mustard together in a drinking glass with a fork until smooth. Add the vinegar and seasonings, and beat with the fork for a few seconds. Pour over the greens just before serving.

A Simple Saltimbocca

Saltimbocca
means "jump
in the mouth."

2	skinless boneless chicken breasts	2
4	slices prosciutto	4
4	fresh sage leaves	4
2 tbsp	olive oil	25 mL
2 tbsp	butter	25 mL
½ cup	white wine or apple juice	125 mL
	Salt	
	Pepper	

Place the chicken breasts on a cutting board, and cover them with plastic wrap or wax paper. Pound the chicken breasts with a mallet, a rolling pin or an empty wine bottle until flattened to a thickness of about ½ inch (1 cm). Remove the plastic wrap or wax paper, and cut a horizontal slit into each chicken breast, about halfway through each breast. Open the slit a bit, and stuff it with two slices of prosciutto and two sage leaves. Have someone repeat with the other chicken breast while you heat the oil and 1 tbsp (15 mL) of the butter in a frypan over medium-high heat. Add the chicken breasts, and cook for 2–3 minutes or until nicely browned on one side. Turn the breasts over, and cook for another 3–4 minutes. Remove the chicken from the pan, and cover the chicken with an upside-down plate to keep it warm. Drain any oil still left in the pan, and return the pan to the heat. Add the white wine, and stir. Cook for 2–3 minutes, then add the remaining 1 tbsp (15 mL) of butter, and stir until melted. Season with salt and pepper, pour over the chicken and serve.

Pumpkin Pudding

¾ cup	whipping cream	175 mL
2	eggs	2
¾ cup	canned puréed pumpkin	175 mL
2 tbsp	white sugar	25 mL
½ tsp	cinnamon	2 mL
	A pinch of nutmeg	

Preheat your oven to 325°F (160°C). Whisk all of the ingredients together in a large bowl until smooth. Pour the mixture into two small greased baking dishes. Place the dishes in a baking pan, and fill the pan with enough hot water to reach halfway up the sides of the dishes. Bake, uncovered, for 40–45 minutes, until the pudding feels firm when touched. Cool to room temperature, and serve with whipped cream or crème fraîche (see page 173).

CHRISTMAS

SWEDISH GLÖGG

A traditional spiced wine recipe.	½ cup	red wine	125 mL
	½ cup	port	125 mL
	¼ cup	vodka	50 mL
		A pinch of cardamom	
		A bit of orange peel	
	2	whole cloves	2
	1	cinnamon stick	1
		(or ½ tsp/2 mL ground cinnamon)	
		A few whole blanched almonds	
		A handful of raisins	

Mix all of the ingredients except the almonds and raisins together in a small pot. Place over low heat, and let the mixture cook until it starts steaming — do not let it boil. Turn the heat off, cover the pot, let the mixture sit for 20 minutes and then strain. Place a few almonds and raisins in a mug, and ladle the glögg over top. Delightful!

Ratatouille

⅓ cup	vegetable oil	75 mL
1	small onion	1
2	cloves garlic	2
1	large eggplant	1
2	sweet red peppers	2
4	tomatoes	4
1	medium zucchini	1
	A sprig of rosemary	
1 cup	red wine or water	250 mL
1 tsp	salt	5 mL

While you heat the oil in a large saucepan over medium-high heat, have someone coarsely chop the onion, garlic, eggplant, peppers, tomatoes, zucchini and rosemary. Add the onions and garlic to the pan, and cook for 2 minutes. Add the eggplant, and cook, stirring, for 3–4 minutes, until it has absorbed most of the oil. Stir in the peppers, tomatoes and zucchini, and cook, stirring, for 5 minutes. Add the rosemary, wine and salt, stir, reduce the heat to low, cover and cook for 2 hours. Check the ratatouille every half hour or so. If all of the liquid has been absorbed, add another ½ cup (125 mL) of water, stir, cover and continue cooking. At the end of the cooking the vegetables will have melted into a gorgeous, thick stew.

GAME HENS WITH OLIVES

Sometimes a
turkey is just too
big.

2 tbsp	vegetable oil	25 mL
2	Cornish game hens	2
1	small onion	1
2	cloves garlic	2
1	bay leaf	1
½ cup	white wine or water	125 mL
12	large green pitted olives	12
1 tbsp	capers	15 mL
1 tsp	dry mustard	5 mL
2 oz	brandy or whisky	60 mL

Heat the oil in a large pot over high heat. Add the hens, and cook until browned all over, about 2 minutes on each side. While you are doing that, have someone chop the onion and garlic. When the hens are browned, add the onion, garlic, bay leaf and wine to the pot. Reduce the heat to medium, add the remaining ingredients and cook for 25–30 minutes, covered. Discard the bay leaf, and serve.

Baked Apples

2	large apples	2
2 tbsp	white sugar	25 mL
	Zest of 1 lemon	
2 tbsp	butter, softened	25 mL

Preheat your oven to 350°F (180°C). Remove the core of the apples, but don't peel them. Place the apples in a greased baking dish, and sprinkle them with the sugar and lemon zest. Dot with butter, and bake, uncovered, for 30 minutes, until soft. Serve with whipped cream, ice cream or crème fraîche (see page 173).

BREADS AND CAKES

*S*poon— rhymes with moon, and tune and lagoon, and of course honeymoon. Spooning was the basis of a lot of old love songs, a pleasant euphemism for cuddling of the so-far-and-no-farther variety, a nice old-fashioned word from a time when more marriages were based on things more practical than lust and less mercenary than joint earning capacity.

My grandmother always asked, "Do you spoon?" when I told her about the most recent of my teenage loves, so I imagine that she, in her time, did it with my grandfather, although any intimate caressing is difficult to imagine since I can't ever recall seeing him without his bowler hat (except when he died and they laid him out on the kitchen table and even then it was on his chest).

But the spooning I remember of my grandmother was another statement of love. She was mean in many ways. I shall never forget her "children's" cocoa, made with cocoa powder and water — no milk, no cream and no sugar. Just a thin mud to drink before going to bed. But in many other ways she was generous — great Yorkshire puddings and, even when I was a six-year-old, "man-sized" slices of beef. Once a week she made cakes and bread. The kitchen smelt wonderful enough to remember even today, and there were bowls on the table, bowls with cake mix in them and bowls with little bits of dough stuck to the sides. There were also spoons, and these were ours to lick and scour clean with our tongues, while my grandfather, who made his own beer and vinegar, carefully sliced thin the onions he grew and sprinkled them with a little salt, a lot of pepper and his brown malt vinegar.

After the nibbling of the spoons, and the picking out of the dough lumps, there was the waiting while the bread and the cakes baked and the onions marinated. This was the story-telling time, with tales about the lifeboat and the shipwrecks and the pigs he raised to win prizes, and it was the time when my grandmother washed the bowls and the tabletop and of course the spoons, even though they were already licked cleaner than any soap and water could make them. When the bread came out of the oven, my grandfather cut it immediately, great thick slices for almost-as-thick slabs of cheese, and over the top we spooned the marinated onions.

Sometimes in summer we spooned thick cream over strawberries fresh from the garden, and sometimes in winter we spooned brown sugar over our morning porridge, brown sugar and more thick cream. We ate a lot of soup (with spoons), and we learned to get the top off a boiled egg with a spoon.

None of this was spooning, not the way my grandmother saw it. But today, years later, whenever I share a spoon in the kitchen, taste somebody else's muffin mix or scrape the jar for the last bit of jam to put on hot biscuits, I feel as if I'm engaging in an act of love.

SAFFRON AND RAISIN CAKE

⅓ cup	raisins	75 mL
⅓ cup	orange juice	75 mL
	A pinch of saffron	
¼ cup	butter, softened	50 mL
½ cup	white sugar	125 mL
4	eggs	4
	A pinch of salt	
1 tbsp	baking powder	15 mL
1 cup	flour	250 mL

Preheat your oven to 350°F (180°C). While one of you sees to making the cake, the other can heat the raisins, orange juice and saffron together in a small saucepan over medium heat. When the orange juice is about to boil, turn off the heat, and let the raisins soak in the mixture until the cake mix is ready. For the cake mix, in a large bowl or food processor cream together the butter and sugar, and then add the eggs, one at a time. Add the salt, baking powder and flour, and stir until everything is smooth. Pour in the raisin mixture, juice and all, and while you are stirring it all together, get someone to butter a 9-inch (1.5 L) round cake pan for you. Pour the batter into the pan, and let it bake for about 20-25 minutes. Or, melt a little butter in a frypan, pour the batter in and let it cook, covered, over low heat for 20 minutes or until the centre is firm when touched. Let the cake cool, and then serve with fresh fruit.

MRS. BEVERLEY BEASLEY'S BANANA BREAD

2	*bananas*	2
1 cup	*buttermilk*	*250 mL*
	(or 1 cup/250 mL milk	
	mixed with the juice of 1 lemon)	
1 tsp	*baking powder*	*5 mL*
⅓ cup	*vegetable oil (not olive)*	*75 mL*
½ cup	*white sugar*	*125 mL*
½ cup	*brown sugar*	*125 mL*
2	*eggs*	2
½ tsp	*cinnamon*	*2 mL*
1 tsp	*vanilla*	*5 mL*
1 ¾ cup	*flour*	*425 mL*
	A pinch of salt	

Mrs. Beasley was a friend of a friend who had a friend in the church choir. She was famous for her banana bread, and word had it (although the recipe never confirmed the rumour) that she used only bananas that were on sale — just a little bit overripe.

*P*reheat your oven to 350°F (180°C). While you deal with the bananas (counting them and peeling them), someone else can start making the cake. Mash the bananas in a large bowl, and then stir in the buttermilk and baking powder. Set the banana mixture aside, and butter a 9- x 5-inch (2 L) loaf tin. To make the cake, combine the oil, sugars and eggs together in a large bowl, and stir until smooth. Add the cinnamon, vanilla, flour and salt, and mix until well combined. Stir in the banana mixture, and pour the batter into the buttered loaf tin. Bake for an hour or until a knife inserted into the cake comes out clean.

Bread and Chocolate!

4	slices really good bread	4
1 ½ oz	dark chocolate, grated	40 g

This isn't really a recipe that two people can prepare together, but it's a wonderful thing to eat together.

*P*reheat a toaster oven or a regular oven to 450°F (230°C). Make two sandwiches: arrange half of the chocolate on one slice of the bread, and place another slice of bread on top. Repeat for the second sandwich. Place the sandwiches on a cookie sheet, and let them toast in the oven for 5 minutes on each side. Remove them from the oven, slice in half and let them cool for a couple of minutes before eating them (otherwise you'll scorch your tongue).

Hot Biscuits in a Hurry

2 cups	flour	500 mL
1 tsp	salt	5 mL
1 ½ tsp	baking powder	7 mL
1 cup	sour cream	250 mL

*P*reheat your oven to 425°F (220°C). Have someone rummage through your cupboards for a wine glass while you mix the dough: stir together the flour, salt and baking powder, and then add the sour cream. Mix it all together until you have a soft, even dough. On a floured surface, pat the dough out to a ¾-inch (2 cm) thickness. Cut the dough into rounds with the wine glass (held upside-down, of course), and place on a lightly greased baking sheet. Bake for 12–15 minutes, and eat immediately. With lots of butter.

Raspberry Coffee Cake

⅓ cup	butter, softened	75 mL
¾ cup	white sugar	175 mL
1	egg	1
½ tsp	vanilla	2 mL
	A pinch of salt	
1 cup	flour	250 mL
1 tsp	baking powder	5 mL
⅓ cup	sour cream or plain yogurt	75 mL
1 cup	raspberries (or any other berry)	250 mL

Fresh raspberries are best, but frozen (even canned) will work if you drain them well and don't mash them up too much.

Topping

2 tbsp	butter, softened	25 mL
2 tbsp	flour	25 mL
½ cup	brown sugar	125 mL

Preheat your oven to 350°F (180°C). Have someone mix together the topping ingredients until crumbly. In the meantime, make the cake batter. Cream together the butter and sugar until smooth and fluffy. Add the egg, vanilla and salt, and stir until well combined. Add the flour and baking powder, stirring until the flour is just mixed in. Then add the sour cream and raspberries. Pour the batter into a greased 9-inch (1.5 L) round cake and sprinkle with the topping. Bake until the centre gives just slightly when touched, about 50 minutes.

Good Ol' Southern Corn Bread

2 tbsp	butter	25 mL
2 tbsp	white sugar	25 mL
3	eggs	3
½ cup	flour	125 mL
1 tbsp	baking powder	15 mL
½ tsp	salt	2 mL
2 cups	cornmeal	500 mL
1 cup	buttermilk	250 mL
	(or 1 cup/250 mL milk	
	mixed with the juice of 1 lemon)	

*P*reheat your oven to 375°F (190°C). While someone else melts the butter, whisk together the sugar and eggs in a large bowl. Add the melted butter, and combine until smooth. Stir in the flour, baking powder and salt, until the flour is just mixed in. Add the cornmeal and buttermilk, and stir until smooth. Pour the batter into a greased 9-inch (2.5 L) square baking pan or a greased frypan, and bake until golden, about half an hour.

Mexican Wedding Cakes

1 cup	walnuts	250 mL
½ cup	butter, softened	125 mL
¼ cup	icing sugar	50 mL
½ tsp	vanilla	2 mL
1 cup	flour	250 mL
	A pinch of salt	
	More icing sugar for decoration	

These are small, nutty shortbread mounds that are simple to make.

*P*reheat your oven to 375°F (190°C). Have someone finely grind the walnuts in a food processor while you cream together the butter and icing sugar in a mixing bowl. Add the vanilla, flour and salt, and then stir in the ground walnuts, mixing until just combined. Pinch off a small piece of dough, and roll it into the size and shape of a golf ball. Place the ball of dough on an ungreased cookie sheet, and press down slightly, to give it a flat bottom. Repeat until you have used up all of the dough. Bake for about 15 minutes. When the cookies have cooled completely, roll them in more icing sugar, and serve.

CURRANT CAKE IN A FRYPAN

1	egg	1
⅔ cup	milk	150 mL
1 tbsp	white sugar	15 mL
1	cup flour	250 mL
	A handful of currants or raisins	
1	lemon	1
2 tsp	baking powder	10 mL
1 tbsp	butter	15 mL

*M*ix together the egg, milk, sugar and flour until smooth (the batter should be fairly thin), and let it sit for 15 minutes. While you add currants to the batter, have someone grate the zest of the lemon and stir it into the batter along with the baking powder. Warm a frypan over low heat, and add the butter, letting it melt. Pour the batter into the frypan, and cover it. Cook for 10–15 minutes, until the top of the batter is just dry. Turn the cake over and let it cook for 5 more minutes. Serve with your favourite tea.

Rosemary and Sun-Dried Tomato Pan Bread

1 ½ cups	flour	375 mL
1 ½ tsp	baking powder	7 mL
½ tsp	baking soda	2 mL
	A pinch of salt	
¼ lb	cold butter, cubed	125 g
	A few sprigs of rosemary	
6	pieces sun-dried tomato	6
2	eggs	2
¼ cup	milk	50 mL
¼ cup	grated Parmesan cheese	50 mL

Preheat your oven to 375°F (190°C). Combine the flour, baking powder, baking soda and salt in a mixing bowl. Use your hands to rub the butter cubes into the flour mixture until you have a coarse, mealy texture. Meanwhile, have someone chop the rosemary and sun-dried tomatoes, and then whisk them together with the eggs, milk and Parmesan cheese. Make a well in the flour mixture, pour the wet ingredients into it and then stir until a ball forms. Pat the dough into a greased ovenproof frypan, and let it rest for 5 minutes before baking it for 25 minutes or until the centre springs back when touched.

DESSERTS

P is for *Pudding*, which is what the English call dessert. It's also for *Partner* and *Passion* and *Play*, but all too often in the kitchen these are pushed aside in favour of *Perfection*. And if you look too hard for *Perfection*, you're doomed to miss an awful lot of just plain *good*.

I go for Passion every time. And Passion, as Doctor Johnson said, is more than four legs in a bed. Culinary Passion is just wanting to create magic in the kitchen, being adventurous and vulnerable, making a few mistakes and not giving a damn, being a bit adventurous and not quite so Prissy.

Take something like Pesto, which a lot of people think you have to have Parmesan cheese (very expensive) and Pine nuts (even more expensive) for, both of which make Pesto Pretty Pricey. But try these alternatives. Use cilantro (some people call it Chinese parsley — it's available all year round, and it's cheap) instead of basil. Use walnuts instead of pine nuts, and use peanut or safflower oil instead of olive oil. The same recipe and technique as you always use — just substitute. Use Asiago cheese instead of Parmesan, and your pesto will cost a third of what it did before. Of course it will taste different, but it will also taste wonderful. Make a pesto out of mint and walnuts and oil and garlic and a little bit of lemon juice (leave out the cheese altogether), and eat it with barbecued lamb or chicken — it's quick, cheap and easy. Surprise yourself.

And while we're on inexpensive alternatives, think about peanut butter and parties. Next time you have a party and want to have everybody asking you for the recipe, try this — it's quick and dirty, and it's great. Put 2 big tablespoons of peanut butter into a bowl, with 2 cloves of garlic chopped fine, and stir in the juice of a big lemon (or 2 small ones). The peanut butter will go thick and stiff, and you now stir in plain yogurt until you have a smooth creamy dip. That's it — an inexpensive version of that Greek dip called hummus, which is made of tahini (ground sesame seeds). But tahini's expensive, and peanut butter ain't. Just try it. It won't cost you much, and — I keep saying this — you'll be surprised.

P is also for *Peas,* which properly cooked are quite capable of engendering passion. In Portugal they put a knob of butter in the bottom of a small saucepan, and then line the inside of the pan with a layer of lettuce leaves. They put the peas inside the nest of leaves with a little mint and another knob of butter, cover them with another leaf, put the lid on and cook them over a medium heat for five minutes. The lettuce leaves go soft and give a nice nutty flavour to the peas, and the butter mixes with the lettuce juice and makes a sauce. You dump them out on a plate, add pepper and salt, and they're gorgeous.

A loaf of good bread, 2 pounds of peas (2 of you can spend a very pleasant half hour shelling them) and a bottle of cold white wine — that's Perfection *and* Passion.

One *P* that you don't want in the kitchen is *Prejudice.* Very few of us are not prejudiced against Prunes, but try this and watch your Prejudice turn to Pride. Next time you roast a chicken, soak a handful of dried prunes in a little hot water for 20 minutes, and then stuff them all into the back end of the chicken (keep the soaking water). Roast the chicken, take it out of the oven, and add the prune water to the chicken juice in the pan. Now add a couple of tablespoons of whisky, boil it fast for 2 minutes, add a little tarragon and call it *Poulet aux Pruneaux d'Agen.*

What's all this got to do with desserts? Most of us are locked into great big slices of cake with icing and chocolate and cream and cherries. We worry about dessert: it has to be right, it has to be complicated and most of the time it's too rich and there's too much of it — more Prohibition to Passion than Prelude. All that sugar will make you sleepy. These few desserts are Pleasant Puddings — simple, easy and comforting. Dessert doesn't have to be the star of the show. *P* is for *Play* as well as *Passion.*

SPANISH-STYLE RICE PUDDING

2 cups	milk	500 mL
1	lemon	1
2 tbsp	butter	25 mL
⅓ cup	white sugar	75 mL
½ tsp	cinnamon	2 mL
	A splash of brandy	
1	egg yolk	1
½ cup	uncooked Arborio (short-grain) rice	75 mL

*P*reheat your oven to 275°F (140°C). Heat the milk in a saucepan over medium heat. In the meantime, have someone grate the zest of the lemon and set it aside. Stir the butter into the warm milk, and bring the milk slowly to a boil. Remove the milk from the heat, and stir in the sugar, lemon zest, cinnamon and brandy. Quickly whisk in the egg yolk, and add the rice. Pour the mixture into a medium buttered baking dish, and put it in the oven. Bake for about 2 hours, checking it once in awhile to make sure all of the liquid hasn't evaporated (if it has, just add a little more milk). Delicious hot or cold.

The Quickie Version of Rice Pudding

2 cups	cooked long-grain rice	500 mL
½ cup	light cream	125 mL
1 tbsp	white sugar	15 mL
	A pinch of nutmeg	

Mix all of the ingredients together, and serve.

Bread Pudding with Bananas

3	bananas	3
2 tbsp	butter, softened	25 mL
4	slices of good bread	4
¾ cup	light cream	175 mL

Preheat your oven to 350°F (180°C). While someone peels and mashes the bananas for you, butter one side of all of the slices of bread. Place two of the slices of bread, buttered side down, in an ungreased baking dish. Spread the mashed bananas over top. Cover the bananas with the remaining two slices of bread, buttered side up. Pour the cream over the whole lot, and bake, uncovered, for about 40 minutes.

Three Ways to Crème Fraîche

#1:

⅓ cup	whipping cream	75 mL
¼ cup	sour cream	50 mL
	A pinch of white sugar	

Whip the cream until stiff. Fold in the sour cream and sugar. Chill for 1 hour, or serve immediately.

#2:

⅓ cup	whipping cream	75 mL
¼ cup	thick yogurt (Greek style)	50 mL
	A pinch of white sugar	

Whip the cream until stiff. Fold in the yogurt and sugar. Chill for 1 hour, or serve immediately.

#3: (THE BEST)

¼ cup	buttermilk	50 mL
	(or 1/4 cup/50 mL milk	
	mixed with 1 tbsp/14 mL lemon juice)	
¾ cup	whipping cream	175 mL

Pour the buttermilk and whipping cream into a jar. Let it sit, at room temperature, for 24 hours. The cream should have thickened to a consistency of sour cream. Serve. Will last two weeks in the jar, refrigerated.

FRENCH APPLE CUSTARD

4	medium apples, soft in texture, like McIntosh or Golden Delicious	4
1	lemon	1
½ cup	butter	125 mL
¾ cup	white sugar	175 mL
3	eggs	3
1 tsp	vanilla	5 mL
2 cups	milk	500 mL
1 ½ cups	flour	375 mL

Preheat your oven to 375°F (190°C). While you peel, core and thinly slice the apples and grate the zest of the lemon, have someone else melt the butter and grease a 9-inch (1.5 L) round cake pan with some of it. Dust the bottom and sides of the greased pan with some of the sugar as well. In a large mixing bowl, cream together the butter and all but 1 tbsp (15 mL) of the remaining sugar until smooth. Beat in the eggs, vanilla and lemon zest, and then add the milk and flour. Lay most of the apples in the bottom of the greased baking pan, and pour the batter over top. Arrange the rest of the apple slices on top, and sprinkle with the last tablespoon (15 mL) of sugar. Bake for about an hour or until the cake has puffed up and the edges start pulling away from the sides of the tin. Serve warm – the cake will sink once removed from the oven – with some Crème Fraîche (see page 173).

Baked Rhubarb

12	stalks fresh rhubarb	12
	(about 4 cups/1 L cubed)	
½ cup	white sugar	125 mL
¼ cup	whipping cream	50 mL

*P*reheat your oven to 375°F (190°C). Cut the rhubarb into small chunks, sprinkle it with sugar and let it sit for half an hour. Put the rhubarb into a greased baking dish, and bake for about 20–25 minutes or until tender. Pour the cream over the rhubarb, and bake for a further 5 minutes. Serve immediately.

Summer Pudding

4–6	thin slices of crustless white bread	4–6
	or sponge cake	
12	strawberries	12
	A handful of blueberries	
	A handful of raspberries	
	A handful of cranberries	
½ cup	white sugar	125 mL

While you line the sides of a small, greased bowl with most of the slices of bread, have someone hull and chop the strawberries. Toss all of the berries together with the sugar, and pour them into the bread-lined bowl. Cover the berries with the remaining bread. Cover the bowl with plastic wrap, and place a plate on top of it. Weigh the plate down with a couple of tins of beans, and refrigerate for 4 hours or so (or even overnight). When you are ready to serve it, invert the pudding onto a plate. Serve with heaps of whipped cream or Crème Fraîche (see page 173).

POACHED PEARS WITH GINGER AND RED WINE

½ cup	white sugar	125 mL
1 cup	red wine	250 mL
½ inch	fresh ginger	1 cm
2	pears	2

While you heat the sugar and red wine together in a pot over medium heat, have someone chop the ginger and peel the pears. Add the ginger and pears to the pot, and reduce the heat to medium-low. Let the pears simmer for 12–15 minutes, and serve with some of the poaching liquid poured over top.

HONEYED PEACHES

½ cup	honey	125 mL
	Juice and zest of ½ lemon	
3 tbsp	water	45 mL
2	peaches	2

While you heat the honey, lemon juice, zest and water in a small saucepan over medium heat, have someone quarter the peaches (leave the skin on). Bring the liquid to a boil, reduce the heat to medium-low and add the peaches. Poach for 5–6 minutes, until tender, and chill. Serve cold with ice cream or crème fraîche (see page 173).

Zabaglione

Just the most sensuous dessert in the world.	4	egg yolks	4
	2 tbsp	white sugar	25 mL
	2 oz	Madeira, Marsala or sherry	50 mL

Heat a small saucepan of water to just below the boiling point. Beat the egg yolks in a bowl until fluffy, and then beat in the sugar and booze. Set the bowl over the hot water (make sure the water doesn't boil), and beat the mixture for 6–8 minutes (you'll probably want to take turns with someone), until it thickens. Pour into tall glasses and eat immediately, or refrigerate and serve very, very cold.

Bananas Flambé

2 tbsp	butter	25 mL
2	bananas	2
2 tbsp	brown sugar	25 mL
	Juice of ½ lemon	
½ tsp	ground ginger or cinnamon	2 mL
1 oz	rum or scotch	25 mL

While someone melts the butter in a frypan over medium heat, halve the bananas lengthwise. Add the brown sugar and lemon juice to the pan, and stir. Lay the bananas flat side down, and cook for 3 minutes. Flip the bananas over, and sprinkle with ginger. Cook for 2 more minutes, and then add the booze. Tilt the pan to let the booze catch a flame (this will only work if you have a gas stove — if it's an electric stove, someone has to have a match), and flambé! Serve when the flame has died out. Great with ice cream.

Pastella

Italian fruit
tempura.

	Vegetable oil	
1 cup	cold water	250 mL
⅔ cup	flour	150 mL
2	medium apples	2
	White sugar	
	Juice of 1 lemon	

Heat 1 inch (2.5 cm) of oil in a saucepan over high heat (if the oil starts smoking, remove it from the heat until it stops, lower the heat a bit and return the saucepan to the heat). While you mix together the water and flour with a fork, have someone core the apples and slice them into ½-inch (1 cm) thick pieces. Dip the apple slices into the batter and then into the hot oil. Cook them, one layer at a time, until golden, turning them over halfway through. Serve immediately, sprinkled with a bit of sugar and lemon juice.

Almond Pine Nut Tarts

	Jam	
12	unbaked 3-inch (7.5 cm) tart shells	12
½ cup	ground almonds	125 mL
⅓ cup	white sugar	75 mL
2	eggs	2
½ cup	butter	125 mL
½ tsp	vanilla	2 mL
3 tbsp	flour	45 mL
1 tsp	baking powder	5 mL
½ cup	pine nuts	125 mL
	Icing sugar	

This recipe makes 12 small tarts. That's a lot for two people, but they freeze easily, and I always like to keep a few on hand for unexpected guests.

Preheat your oven to 350°F (180°C). While you spread a thin layer of jam (raspberry is especially nice), on the bottom of each tart shell, have someone whiz together the almonds, sugar, eggs, butter and vanilla in a food processor until smooth. Add the flour and baking powder, and whiz again briefly. Fill the tarts with the almond mixture, and sprinkle a few pine nuts on top of each one. Bake for about 20 minutes. Let the tarts cool, sprinkle them with icing sugar and serve.

BBQ Fruit Skewers

Use fresh fruit if you can, but canned will do in a pinch.	1	peach	1
	½	pineapple	½
	2–4	wooden skewers	2–4
	½ cup	plain yogurt	125 mL
		A sprig of mint	

While you slice the peach into bite-sized pieces, have someone do the same with the pineapple. Soak the skewers in water for a few minutes. Thread the fruit onto the skewers in any old order, and place them on a hot grill (or even under your toaster oven broiler) for 1 minute on each side. Serve with a dollop of yogurt and a mint leaf.

Oranges with Grated Chocolate

2	oranges	2
1 oz	good dark, semi-sweet chocolate	25 g
	A pinch of cinnamon or nutmeg	

Cut the peel off the oranges, and slice them. Arrange the slices on a plate. Grate the chocolate over top, and serve with a sprinkle of cinnamon.

CARAMEL APPLES ON PUFF PASTRY

1	egg	1
2 tbsp	milk	25 mL
1	piece (4 oz/100 g) frozen puff pastry, thawed	1
1 tsp	white sugar	5 mL
2	medium apples	2
1 tbsp	fresh lemon juice	15 mL
⅓ cup	white sugar	75 mL
¼ cup	whipping cream	50 mL
1 tbsp	Calvados or brandy	15 mL

Preheat your oven to 350°F (180°C). While one of you sees to the pastry, the other can prepare the apples and caramel. For the pastry, stir the egg and milk together. On a floured surface, roll the pastry into a square that is ¼ inch (5 mm) thick, and brush with the egg wash. Sprinkle the 1 tsp (5 mL) of sugar over top of the pastry, and cut into two triangles. Bake on a greased baking sheet for 15 minutes or until golden. To prepare the apples, peel, core and cut each apple into ¼-inch (5 mm) wedges, and toss them in the lemon juice and 1 tbsp (15 mL) of the ⅓ cup (75 mL) sugar. To make the caramel, place the remaining sugar in a heavy-bottomed pan over high heat, and let it cook until it turns medium brown. The caramel is extremely hot, so be careful not to splash yourself. Remove the caramel from the heat, and slowly stir in the cream and Calvados. Toss the apples in this sauce, return the saucepan to medium heat and cook until the apples are soft and the sauce has thickened. This will take about 10 minutes. Serve warm apples over pastry.

INDEX

SALADS

*D*inner takes longer to cook than supper. And longer to shop for. Once you get the dinner bug (it starts on Sunday when you decide that Friday would be a good night to have the Johnsons to dinner), there's no escape until you finally get them out of the door ("Lovely evening. So glad you could come . . .") and either fight or collapse into one another's arms. Or both.

You think *you've* got it bad, with a week of worry ("Do they like lamb?" "Didn't they say something once about tofu?"). But they've got it too ("Is this going to be formal?" "Remember what happened when we went to the Wilsons?"). Dinner *looms.* All week it's a threat: "How do you know when an avocado's ripe?" "Will the strawberries keep?" "Did their kid really set fire to the school?" "And whatever you do, *don't talk about Palestine . . .*"

Supper's easier. Nobody panics if it's late or if the wine's the wrong year (or even the wrong colour), and people who eat supper seem to like helping with the dishes.

Supper is a one-plate meal (the best suppers are one-pot), and when you've mopped up the last of the gravy (sauce is for *dinner*), you're ready for salad or cheese or a little fruit. Supper for guests is always lots — lots of potatoes or rice or couscous, lots of reaching across the table, lots of belt-loosening. Second helpings are in order — so is asking for them. Ideally (although sometimes people go for thirds), there will always be a bit left over for

Cooking for Two